Lord Ja
History
where he
became P
Formerly
Member of Parliament for West Edinburgh and is also the author of *Motive for
a Mission: The Story Behind Rudolf Hess's
Flight to Britain.* His uncle was Lord
David Douglas-Hamilton, whose diaries
of the war years have made this book
possible.

'Scrupulously researched . . . and skil-
fully put together to recreate the period,
the comradeship and the grimness of life
on a tiny beleagured island . . . a vivid
picture of one of the greatest air battles
in history, in which a tiny and hungry
force, ill-served with supplies, struggled
to supremacy.'

THE SCOTSMAN

'A sensitive account of one man's view of
the war . . . Reading this book is like
being there, in the cockpit and on the
ground.'

THE STANDARD

'Full of authority . . . brimming with
personal experiences and insights . . . an
outstanding narrative . . . captivating
reading.'

THE TIMES (of Malta)

THE AIR BATTLE FOR
MALTA

Lord James
Douglas-Hamilton MP

Introduction by Laddie Lucas

Hamlyn Paperbacks

THE AIR BATTLE FOR MALTA
ISBN 0 600 20659 9

First published in Great Britain 1981
by Mainstream Publishing Company (Edinburgh) Ltd
Hamlyn Paperbacks edition 1982
Copyright ©1981 by James Douglas-Hamilton
Introduction © P.B. (Laddie) Lucas CBE, DSO, DFC

Hamlyn Paperbacks are published by
The Hamlyn Publishing Group Ltd,
Astronaut House,
Feltham,
Middlesex, England

Printed and bound in Great Britain by
Cox & Wyman Ltd, Reading

The photographs which appear on the front cover are
reproduced by courtesy of the Imperial War Museum,
London, and (inset) the U.S. National Archives.

To those in the Royal Air Force who gave their lives
in the Second World War
and
to their families

"He either fears his fate too much
Or his deserts are small
That dares not put it to the touch
To gain or lose it all"

James Graham, Marquis of Montrose

Contents

Acknowledgments

THE author and Publishers wish to thank the following, who have kindly given permission for the use of copyright material:—

Ernest Benn Ltd., for extract from *Grace under Malta*, by Sybil Dobbie; Mrs. Diana Cameron for extracts from 603 Squadron Diary, written by Squadron Leader Lord David Douglas-Hamilton and her father, Squadron Leader Bill Douglas D.F.C; Cassell and Company Limited for extracts from Volumes II and IV of the *History of the Second World War* by Sir Winston Churchill; William Collins and Company Limited for extract from *The Rommel Papers*, by B.H. Liddell Hart; Peter Davies for extracts from *Tattered Battlements, A Malta Diary* by a Fighter Pilot; Robert Hale Limited for extract from *Malta, The Triumphant Years*, by G. Hogan; Heinemann for extract from the *Memoirs of Lord Ismay;* Her Majesty's Stationery Office for extracts from *The Air Battle of Malta*, the official Account of the R.A.F. in Malta, June 1940 to November 1942, published by the Ministry of Information, from the *History of the Second World War* Volume II by Captain S.W. Roskill, and from the *History of the Second World War* Volume III by General Playfair; Hodder and Stoughton for extracts from *The Unconquered Isle, The Story of Malta G.C.,* by Ian Hay; from *Briefed to Attack, Malta's part in African Victory*, by Air Vice Marshal Sir Hugh Lloyd, and from *The Siege within the Walls, Malta 1940-1943* by Stewart Perowne; Jarrolds and Lawrence Pollinger Ltd., for extracts from *Where no Angels Dwell*, by Air Vice Marshal Sandy Johnstone, D.F.C., and from *Spitfires over Malta*, by Paul Brennan and Ray Hesselyn; William Kimber and Company Limited for extracts from *The Battle of Malta*, by Joseph Attard, from *The Fighter Aces of the R.A.F. 1939-1945* by E.C.R. Baker, from *The Memoirs of Field Marshal Kesselring*, and from *Faith Hope and Charity, Three Planes against an Air Force,* by Kenneth Poolman.

Mr. and Mrs. Dermot McDermid for extracts from the papers of Group Captain Arthur Donaldson, D.S.O.

D.F.C., A.F.C., Oxford University Press for extracts from the *Struggle for Crete,* by G. McD. G. Stewart; Mrs. Brian Power, for extracts from Lord David Douglas-Hamilton's Diary and papers; The Public Record Office for extracts from the Prime Minister's papers; for extracts with the gracious permission of Her Majesty the Queen from the Royal Archives and for extracts with the permission of *The Times of Malta.*

The author also wishes to thank The Rt. Hon. Francis Pym M.C., Geoffrey Pattie, Air Commodore Henry Probert M.B.E. and Mr. McDonald of the Air Historical Branch, Mrs. Brian Power, O.B.E., Duke of Hamilton, The Rt. Hon. Earl of Selkirk, KT., G.C.M.G., G.B.E., A.F.C., Paul Evans, D.F.C., Group Captain Cahill, D.S.O., Group Captain Jack Satchell D.S.O., Denis Barnham, D.F.C., Professor Reg Jones C.B., C.B.E., Ian Ritchie, Miss Park, Sir Edward Brown, M.B.E., Dr. Bevan Jones, Air Vice Marshal Frank Dodd C.B.E, D.S.O., D.F.C., A.F.C., Lord deL'Isle V.C., K.G. G.C.M.G., Sir John Colville, C.B., C.V.O., Miss Eliza Oxley, Harold Lind, Charles Wild, Owen Dudley Edwards, Dr. Eugene Pugatch, the U.S. Naval Historical Center in Washington D.C., the U.S. Embassy, the U.S. National Archives, the Imperial War Museum, the R.A.F. Museum, and the House of Commons Library for their assistance.

The three Spitfire pilots who give the author invaluable accounts, to whom he is very grateful are:

Laddie Lucas C.B.E., D.S.O., D.F.C., one of the first Spitfire pilots in Malta.

Tony Holland D.F.C., the remaining survivor of the Spitfire pilots of 603 Squadron flown off the U.S.S. *Wasp,* and Air Vice Marshal Sandy Johnstone, C.B., D.F.C., one of the last Spitfire pilots to arrive in Malta, when the circumstances had changed.

The missing link in the story was provided by the late Group Captain Arthur Donaldson, D.S.O., D.F.C., A.F.C. He was present during the last massive confrontation between the Luftwaffe and the Spitfire pilots in October, 1942. Curiously only one fighter pilot received the Victoria Cross in the Second World War, but Arthur Donaldson probably came as close to winning it as any.

The bulk of the story is based on the 603 Squadron Diary and the personal Diary of its Commander, Squadron Leader Lord David Douglas-Hamilton, along with other material provided by his widow, Mrs. Brian Power, as this covered the period when Malta's very existence hung in the balance, and the battle fought on 10th May 1942 was the turning point in the Air Battle for Malta.

Had it not been for the Diaries, in which he paid tribute to the Spitfire pilots who served with him, David might have taken his place among the countless unknown warriors of the Second World War. As it happened he was one of the only four brothers in the Royal Air Force all of whom became professional flying instructors and Squadron Commanders. His three older brothers became Wing Commanders and then Group Captains, but of the four of them David was the only brother to command a Spitfire squadron at the height of the Battle. He was a patriot and a leader and therein lay his greatness.

There were of course, countless courageous men and women, perhaps millions whose contribution in the Second World War will never be known. If it makes it easier to understand what was done by so many, by telling the story of a key battle as seen through the eyes of one man and a few of his friends, then this book will have served its purpose.

Introduction by

P.B. (LADDIE) LUCAS, DSC DFC CBE

THE battle for Malta in the Second World War, which ebbed and flowed with varying intensity from early in 1940 to the first weeks of 1943, will rank in history as one of the great defensive—and strategic—operations of all time. Yet, even now, little is known about it.

There are three reasons for this. First, size. Malta is a diminutive island with a small population, set in a large sea. The public mind has never been able to reconcile its size with its strategic importance.

Second, numbers. Relatively few combatants took part in the various phases of the battle: fewer still were involved in all of them. There have never been many who could say with truth, "I was there".

Third, the record. There is a striking paucity of first-rate and authoritative writing about it. What there is is often incomplete, and based on material taken at second hand. It is remarkably unmoving. To those who lived through the sombre days of 1942, when success and disaster shouted at one another across a terrible divide, much of it lacks credence and conviction.

We did not have an Alan Moorehead, a Quentin Reynolds, an Ed Murrow, or an Alexander Clifford to embellish our fluctuating fortunes; nor was there a Richard Hillary among the few Squadrons to immortalise the pilots' hopes and fears. By comparison with the highly dramatised and widely reported campaigns which embraced large armies, vast land tracts, major areas of population, Malta may at the time have appeared to be little more than a pin-prick in the global conflict. It is the antithesis of the truth. In fact, the island's significance in the course and history of World War II was profound.

Malta, lying like some wounded and enraged beast of prey along the Germans' supply routes, was a constant menace to General Rommel and his Afrika Corps. Its presence inhibited his Desert campaign. It hindered the unfolding of Hitler's grand strategy in the Middle East. It forced Kesselring to commit a front-line strength of six hundred aircraft—fighters and bombers—in Sicily and Southern Italy. Goering's Luftwaffe could well have used these aircraft on the Western Front.

Had Malta fallen to the enemy in April or early May, 1942—which it might very well have done—the effect on the Allies' plans for North Africa would have been catastrophic. The Desert campaign would have been harmed. The invasion of Sicily and Italy would have been thwarted or, at best, delayed. The timing and success of the Normandy landing in 1944, and the subsequent advance through France and the Low Countries into Germany, would have been seriously affected. In short, a chain reaction of quite hideous proportions would have attended the garrison's fall.

History may well say that Hitler's loss of the Malta battle—and the High Command's appalling misjudgment of the island's resilience—was no less crucial to his ultimate defeat than his earlier failure to quell the strength of Fighter Command in the Battle of Britain.

*   *   *   *   *

The memories of the island's wartime story remain sharp.

I still have in my mind the scene a few of us witnessed one sunny, late winter's morning in February as we arrived in Malta to open our account. Stan Turner, the widely-experienced Canadian squadron and wing-leader, Raoul Daddo-Langlois, Bob Sergeant, Tex Putnam, a compatriot of Turner's, and I, had just stepped out of a Sunderland flying boat, which had brought us through a disturbed, electric night from Gibraltar along the length of the western Mediterranean to the island. We were fresh from flying well-maintained Spitfires in Fighter Command in England and more than a little blasé about it. As we walked away from the jetty beside the lapping waters of Kalafrana Bay and made our way to the mess for breakfast, the air-raid sirens started wailing.

In a few moments we looked up and there, clawing and

clambering up through the early morning haze, were four, clapped-out, antiquated Hurricane IIs, struggling for height, in an old-fashioned Vic formation. They couldn't have been at more than three or four thousand feet as they passed overhead. We discovered afterwards that it was all the defence could muster out of the ten or twelve supposedly serviceable aircraft on the island. The Spitfires had yet to arrive.

Six or eight thousand feet above our quartet, flying their beautifully loose, open formation, were three sections of four Messerschmitt 109Fs, sweeping in fast and confidently, well ahead of the incoming raid. The customary "blue note" of their Daimler Benz, fuel-injection engines, was transmitting its ominous message to the ground. It was a chilling spectacle.

We flew those old Hurricanes against the hordes of 109Fs for a month before the first Spitfires began to filter through from the carriers. It was a daunting interlude and taught us what the pilots had been enduring day after day during the last few, tortuous months. Visions of another Crete began to unsettle our sleep.

※   ※   ※   ※   ※

There are, in my experience, several certain ways of getting to know a man as he really is. One is by flying and fighting alongside him in an air battle in which the odds are unfairly weighted in favour of the enemy. Here the evidence of character is laid so bare that true worth cannot be hidden: shams do not long remain undetected.

Lord David Douglas-Hamilton, the author's uncle, and I had a special relationship in Malta. In peace, sport (he was a boxer and I a golfer) had made a bond between us. Now, his Spitfire squadron and mine were based on the same small, bomb-pocked airfield at Takali. For four unequal, torrid months, after he had flown 603 Squadron off the United States' carrier, *Wasp*, into the island in an outstanding Anglo-American operation, his pilots and ground crews, and 249's, lived close together in conditions which none of us would wish to see repeated.

David wasn't a brilliant, individual fighter pilot in the

sense of shooting down a lot of German aircraft. He hadn't the mercurial qualities of Beurling, Plagis, Nash, Brennan, MacQueen, Hurst or Hesselyn, who flashed and twinkled about the sky, slipping, swiftly and unseen, into an opportunist position here or sliding trickily out of a nasty predicament there. David was solid and steady and all for the Squadron. He thought little of himself. My guess is that he denied himself chances that others might seize them. Had I been a junior officer or sergeant in 603, and new to the squadron, I would have felt safe with him because he would be thinking about the other pilots— and, perhaps, me in particular. If I got shot down, and survived, I would know the chances were it had been through my own stupidity and not because he had forgotten about those flying with him. He didn't make that kind of mistake, trying to lift his own personal score. There was a benign assertiveness about him which kept the younger pilots feeling he was acting for them, not only in the office of Squadron Commander, but also as guardian.

Moreover, his team approach enabled him to work well with the ground controllers and trust them. There were good reasons for doing so, for throughout the late winter, spring and summer of 1942, we had the services of Group Captain A. B. Woodhall, the outstanding fighter controller of the war. He had learnt the art the hard way—with Douglas Bader at Duxford and Tangmere during and just after the Battle of Britain. Woody, by his masterminding of the operations from the ground, took us by the hand in the air and set up the opportunities.

David Douglas-Hamilton's leadership—and, indeed, that of Stan Grant, my exceptional predecessor in 249— was never seen to better purpose than during the great air battles of 9 and 10 May 1942. These marked the turning point of the campaign, the two historic days when the eventual fate of the Luftwaffe was first scribbled on the wall. Within forty-eight hours, thanks to a brilliantly-conceived reinforcing operation, involving all three Services and, once again, the US Navy's carrier, *Wasp*, Kesselring took a punch on the solar plexus from which he and his air force never fully recovered. Saved by the bell, he got to his feet again with his usual courage and fought on vigorously for several more rounds. But thereafter he knew he couldn't win; an invasion wasn't on, whereas we, for our part, began to feel that, given patience, resolution and a stroke or two of gamblers' luck, relief would eventually come. It wouldn't be tomorrow or next week, but it might possibly be next month. When you have been living for weeks on dwindling rations of food, ammunition and fuel, and you know from what *isn't* being said that you are pretty close to the last gasp, it's a great thing to feel you may, after all, survive.

It is much to the advantage of the record that, in these hard days, David kept a careful, daily diary of his squadron's activities. Apart from the benefit which history derives, his graphic accounts tell us much about the character of the man— his naked honesty and the balance of his judgment. Their authority is undoubted and they provide, at first hand, a realistic portrayal of the unrelenting duel in the sun.

*   *   *   *   *

Much has been made of the gunning of pilots, as they floated to safety in their parachutes; but it was the exception to prove the rule of hard, clean, ruthless fighting in the air. I personally saw it happen but once— to a fine Rhodesian pilot in 249 named Douggie Leggo. Bounced out of the sun by the German ace, Neuhoff, whom 249 then shot down, Leggo rolled his Spitfire onto its back and parted company. His parachute opened immediately. As he descended earthwards, a lone Messerschmitt, appearing seemingly from nowhere, sprayed the canopy with tracer bullets in a callous gesture of murder. It was over in seconds. There was no chance of retaliation.

No discipline will hold the blind fury of a squadron which has witnessed such cruelty to a comrade. I knew it could only be a question of days before one of the pilots, surreptitiously, would find a chance of levelling the score. It came within a week. A Junkers 88 had been shot down south west of the island. The aircraft had ditched in the sea and now the crew of three were in a dinghy ten miles or so from Delimara Point. Their chances of being picked up must have been good. The sea was calm and sparkling. A Dornier 24 would have had no trouble making a landing. As we headed home for Takali, my eye caught sight of a single Spitfire away to my left, at the bottom of a shallow, fast dive, heading straight for the dinghy. A sustained burst of fire sent geysers of sea water creeping up on the tiny, inflated boat. Not content with one run, the pilot pulled up into a tight climbing turn to the left and dived again. In war, one bad act will always beget another. . . .

❊   ❊   ❊   ❊   ❊

In the summer of 1942, with the extent of the odds against us, we were dependent upon one another in the air for survival.

In combat it was a basic rule that aircraft flew in pairs, loosely in line abreast, and three or four hundred yards apart. The eyes of the pilot to the right were responsible for everything which went on to the left. The pilot flying on the left was concerned only with the sky to the right. With each man looking inwards towards his mate, there could be no blind spots; all was covered. The pair was fundamental to our existence.

A section of four Spitfires, flying in line abreast, was based on two pairs; two sections of four aircraft on four pairs; a Squadron of three sections, the customary complement, depended on six pairs—twelve aircraft all in touch and relying, for their safety and their opportunities, upon the individual pair.

And if, in a melée, one became separated from the rest, there was but one rule to observe: find another Spitfire in the vast wide sky and join up quickly in line abreast. You might not know who was in it, or, if it had no markings, from which squadron it came. It did not matter. You were a pair again, and both of you would know the lines and the cues like professional actors on stage. There was no need for rehearsal. Reactions were spontaneous. Each pilot, knowing the Malta form, relied, in surrendered faith, upon the other.

Many were the times when, outnumbered but not out-manoeuvred, a 249 pilot would find himself, after a fight, depending for his saftety on an aircraft from 603. The Squadrons lived together in dedicated rivalry, each trying to better the other; but when it came to survival we were as one.

*   *   *   *   *

In October 1942, Kesselring made a final attempt to destroy Malta's fighter defence. In telling this part of the island story, James Douglas-Hamilton is fortunate to have had recourse to the first-hand writing of Group Captain Arthur Donaldson. Like the four Douglas-Hamilton brothers, Jack, Teddy and Arthur, all commanded squadrons in the Royal Air Force. It was a signal family achievement that each of the Donaldsons won the DSO.

Arthur Donaldson's personal account of the final Malta blitz is of capital importance for one governing reason. It marks the switch in tactics from the purely defensive role of the spring and summer to the forward and immensely successful offensive interceptions of the autumn. By then, as a result of reinforcing operations from the carriers, the aircraft strength on the island had built up dramatically to levels which David Douglas-Hamilton and the other Squadron Commanders had never dreamt of, let alone known.

Defensive battles had still to be fought to the death over the island; but the enemy was now being met head on over the sixty-mile stretch of water between Malta and Sicily, and even over the Sicilian mainland itself. It was a dramatic change in direction from the Summer. By 20 October the defeat of the Luftwaffe was complete.

It was a fitting end to one of the greatest air battles in history, which the author recounts with commendable directness, colour and authority.

LADDIE LUCAS
November 1980

Part I

By God's help, Malta will not weaken.

General Dobbie, Governor of Malta
21 January 1941

Chapter One
THE STRUGGLE FOR SURVIVAL

ON 11 June 1940, amid the brilliance of the sunlight, the calm of the Maltese way of life was broken by the wail of the sirens and the splintering crash of bombs exploding. Emboldened by the collapse of France to the forces of the Third Reich, Italy had just declared war on Britain.

For the Italians and their allies Malta was both a natural and a vital target. Lying within only sixty to sixty-five miles of the large Italian air bases in Sicily, the island dominated the key strategic centre of the Mediterranean. While the British held Malta the Royal Navy could fight its way through the Mediterranean, saving fifteen thousand miles and forty-five days on the journey round the Cape.

Years of neglect by the British Government, however, had left Malta almost entirely without an air defence. The British Cabinet, wrongly imagining that the French fleet would help to ensure the safeguarding of sea routes to Malta—so vital to an island less than half self-sufficient in food—had underestimated the need for protection. Now France lay prostrate before the advance of Germany's Panzer Divisions, her fleet in no position to shield the convoy traffic to Malta through the Western Mediterranean.

On that June day, while thousands of miles away all Hurricanes and Spitfires were being held in reserve for the imminent Battle of Britain, the defenders of Malta did not have the benefit of a single Royal Air Force fighter aircraft. And yet if Malta were to fall into enemy hands, the consequences would be unthinkable. Not only would the Mediterranean route be closed to British shipping: there would be no staging base for aircraft reinforcements for Egypt, and British submarines and aircraft would be severely hampered in their ability to disrupt Axis supply lines.

Every member of the garrison in Malta knew that the island would have to be fought for to the very end. The Maltese civilians also believed the garrison would fight back with absolute resolve and felt totally committed to the struggle.

Historically, the Maltese and the British had enjoyed a close relationship ever since the days of Napoleon Bonaparte when the superior attitudes of the French dictator's supporters caused Maltese sympathies to lie with the Admiral Lord Nelson, commanding the British fleet. There then began an era of friendship between the Maltese and the British, with the Maltese economy benefitting from the British presence. English came to be used as the language in the law courts and often in business dealings, and down the years to 1940 many Maltese joined both the Royal Malta Artillery and the King's Own Malta Regiment.

With one notable exception the Maltese had enjoyed an atmosphere of peacefulness for nearly a thousand years. Their island had previously been visited by the Phoenicians, a seafaring race, and by the Romans before the life of Christ. Saint Paul of Tarsus had made a surprise visit there when the Roman ship in which he was held prisoner was shipwrecked, and during his stay had converted many to Christianity, the religion to which the Maltese have adhered ever since.

In about 1100 the Arabs came, followed by the Normans and Aragonese. Then arrived one of the most striking periods of Malta's history, during the Crusades. The Knights of Jerusalem, having been compelled to retreat from the Holy Land, eventually came to Malta. There they erected magnificent buildings and fortifications, and what followed is known by every Maltese schoolboy.

In 1565 the first Great Siege of Malta began, with the Maltese and the few hundred Knights of St John of Jerusalem under their Commander la Valette holding the island against the thirty thousand Turkish invaders.

At the mouth of the Grand Harbour of the city, now named Valletta, had been the fort of St Elmo. When the sixty Knights holding out were surrounded, la Valette refused to give them permission to evacuate. They died fighting to the last man, but their stand had helped to save Malta, giving la Valette the time he needed for his relief ships to arrive, breaking the siege.

Just as that victory was to lead to an even greater success at the Battle of Lepanto in 1571 when the Papal, Venetian and Spanish fleets destroyed the Turkish fleet, so too the Air Battle for Malta almost four centuries later would one way or another decide the outcome of the struggle for North Africa and the Middle East.[1]

*   *   *   *   *

The Great Siege of 1565, which had ended in a glorious victory, remained in the national memory. But that morning, in 1940, as they watched in dismay the bombs hurtling down from the Italian Cants, killing civilians and shattering buildings, few of the Maltese could imagine that they were about to undergo a Second Great Siege. Fewer still could have believed that in the course of the months that lay ahead fourteen thousand tons of bombs would be dropped on the 143 square miles of Malta and Gozo.

The Governor, General Dobbie, did what was required of him in the circumstances. He issued an Order of the Day which was infused with a deep religious fervour. It read:

> The decision of His Majesty's Government to fight until our enemies are defeated will be heard with the greatest satisfaction by all ranks of the Garrison of Malta.
>
> It may be that hard times lie ahead of us, but I know that however hard they may be, the courage and determination of all ranks will not falter, and that with God's help we will maintain the security of this fortress.
>
> I call on all Officers and other ranks humbly to seek God's help, and then in reliance on Him to do their duty unflinchingly.[2]

He worked hard to transform the island nation into a

people ready to keep fighting to the finish. Air-raid shelters had been and would be prepared, and arrangements **were** made to rehouse the homeless and to introduce rationing, ensuring that Malta built up nine months reserves of all essential supplies. Above all the three Armed Services, supported by an enduring people, were to resist this onslaught to the uttermost. All that stood in the way of the Italian Air Force were the Maltese and British manning a few anti-aircraft guns, and four Gladiator aircraft.

A few weeks earlier the British aircraft carrier *Glorious* had sailed from Malta, leaving behind some packing cases containing the parts of four Sea-Gladiator biplane fighters. The Air Officer Commanding, Air Commodore Maynard borrowed them from the Navy. His personal assistant, Flight Lieutenant George Burges, and Flying Officer W.J. Woods learned how to fly them.

On that day in June 1940, when they were first sent up to intercept the Italian bombers, a Macchi 200 fighter attacked Wood's Gladiator. In his Combat Report he wrote:

> . . . I suddenly heard machine-gun fire from behind me. I immediately went into a steep left-hand turn and saw a single-engine fighter diving and firing at me. For quite three minutes I circled as tightly as possible and got the enemy in my sight. I got a good burst in, full deflection shot, and he went down in a steep dive with black smoke pouring from his tail. I could not follow him down, but he appeared to go into the sea.[3]

One of the four Gladiators would be damaged, and the three which remained showed that they would be a force to be reckoned with: in due course they were to be renamed affectionately as "Faith, Hope and Charity". Normally, though, they were only able to attack stragglers as the Italian air force had the advantage in numbers and speed.

On Saturday, 22 June an S79 bomber appeared over Malta on a reconnaissance mission, and was attacked by

Flight Lieutenant Burges. As he fired he saw the bomber's port and starboard engines burst into flames, and in Valletta and Sliema the Maltese near the seafront could see the burning aircraft plunging towards the sea. It was followed by two Italian airmen, floating down at the end of their parachutes. Malta's first prisoners of war had arrived.[4]

By the end of June seventy civilians had been killed by the bombs, and a few Hurricanes appeared in Malta. In July more Hurricanes were taken in the small British aircraft carrier *Argus* to within four hundred miles of Malta, and flew the rest of the distance. Soon these aircraft became the principal defence force, operating from Luqa aerodrome, overlooking the Grand Harbour. The other two aerodromes were Takali and Hal Far, the last of which accommodated the Gladiators and the Fleet Air Arm Swordfish.

As early as July 1940 Swordfish from Hal Far bombed oil depots in Sicily. With the gradual extension of Malta's offensive role, more than a thousand Maltese joined the Royal Air Force and many other Maltese became anti-aircraft gunners or joined the Navy: the ferocity of the attack had thrown the Maltese and the soldiers, sailors and airmen together in a most remarkable way. They knew they would have to work together closely to make the island fortress secure, to fend off the threat of invasion and to survive, and they accepted their lot with spirit and fortitude.

Hardly any Maltese had been known to sympathise with Mussolini's Fascism, and such persons were speedily arrested and detained after Italy's declaration of war. They were treated with courtesy, and most of them were taken to Kenya. There was little criticism of these detentions.[5]

The Maltese regarded the Governor, General Dobbie, with awe and admiration. He was often seen making his way around Valletta, threading his route through the debris of the ruined houses strewn across the streets, and encouraging the civilians. He told them with sincerity that all would come right if they worked hard and kept their faith in the Lord. Under his orders underground chambers were hewn out of the rock for storing food, and the Maltese were advised to sleep below ground in deep rock shelters and in the catacombs, so as to minimise casualties.

In spite of constant bombing, convoys to Malta, escorted by the British fleet, continued to bring supplies, including food, ammunition and fuel. In Air Commodore Maynard's office there was a chart, which gave details of the permissible amount of fuel to be allocated to aircraft each week.[6] Under siege conditions the Defence Forces and the Maltese would have to make a little go a long way.

Throughout the late Summer and Autumn, the bombing of the aerodromes and dockyards continued, but reinforcements continued to arrive.

On 6 October the Prime Minister, Winston Churchill, sent a memorandum to General Ismay, the Chief of Staff: "Whenever the Fleet is moving from Alexandria to the Central Mediterranean, reinforcements should be carried to Malta, which I consider to be in grievous danger at the present time."[7] He and other Ministers in the War Cabinet considered that Malta must become a base of offensive operations against the Axis.

In August more Hurricanes had been flown off the *Argus,* but in November a further attempt met with tragedy. Fourteen aircraft took off from the carrier, but the headwind against them was so strong that nine out of the fourteen ran out of fuel. Never again would such risks be taken without adequate preparation.[8]

That same month Malta-based aircraft were more fortunate, when reconnaissance missions were carried out from Hal Far. One of the pilots was Wing Commander Adrian Warburton, who was tall, fair and of slight build, and who became something of a legend on the island. He took photographs from his Beaufighter at very low levels, sometimes at five thousand feet or below.

On 10 November Warburton flew over the Italian naval base at Taranto, and to his astonishment saw five battleships, fourteen cruisers and twenty-seven destroyers. In spite of the anti-aircraft fire he circled and went back, taking photographs for a second time. Then in order to make absolutely certain, he went back a third time, and by a miracle his aircraft missed the flak. He arrived back at Hal Far, where a magnificent set of prints were developed.[9]

Early the next day, 11 November, the British carrier *Illustrious* sent an aeroplane to Hal Far to collect the photographs which showed the five Italian battleships nestling within Taranto Harbour. At 8.49 and 9.30 p.m. that night two strike forces of twelve and nine Swordfish, carrying torpedoes, took off from the *Illustrious*, 180 miles south east of Taranto. Surprise was absolute, and for the loss of only two Swordfish, the battleship *Cavour* was torpedoed, later being beached and abandoned. The battleships *Duilio* and *Littorio* were seriously damaged. Two auxiliary ships were badly damaged, and two cruisers had taken a heavy list. In the course of those two attacks, half the Italian battle fleet had been put out of action.[10]

Information like that brought back by Warburton was invaluable before attacks were launched. Future attacks by Wellington, Blenheim and Baltimore bombers on Axis ports and convoys were executed after hundreds of arduous reconnaissance missions over the Mediterranean, Italy, Sicily, Sardinia and Tunisia. Sometimes the photo-reconnaissance pilots' information was far from welcome. Early in January 1941 a reconnaissance flight yielded the menacing news that the Luftwaffe was arriving on Sicilian airfields with many bombers—Junkers 87s and 88s.

On 10 January the *Illustrious*, whose Swordfish had inflicted such damage on the Italian fleet, listed into the Grand Harbour, having been seriously damaged by Luftwaffe divebombers. The convoy with her was quickly unloaded, and the harbour gunners prepared for a powerful assault. On 16 January over seventy German bombers attacked, seeking revenge on the carrier.

The Harbour gunners had prepared a box barrage so that the bombers would have to fly through a wall of fire, and a fighter force of four Hurricanes and three Fulmars was scrambled. The harbour barrage was more intense than the Maltese had ever known, with bombs exploding all round the *Illustrious*, although only one struck home.

So determined were the RAF fighter pilots that one of them flying a Fulmar followed a German bomber right through the gunners' barrage. An artillery officer said:

I can still see clearly a German bomber diving through that terrific curtain of steel, followed by a Fulmar. The bomber dropped his bomb and proceeded to sneak his way out through the harbour entrance only a few inches above the water. He was so low that he had to rise to clear the breakwater, which is only some fifteen feet high. He was obviously wobbling badly, and as he rose the Fulmar pilot shot him down into the sea on the far side of the breakwater. The Fulmar pilot then landed at his airfield, and later I received a message from him to say that he did not think much of our barrage! However he never flew that particular plane again, so badly was it damaged. Ten German aircraft had been shot down, five by the Harbour gunners and five by the fighter pilots.[11]

On 18 January some eighty Luftwaffe bombers attacked Hal Far and Luqa in an attempt to neutralise the fighter defence. The Luftwaffe lost eleven aircraft, seven to fighters and four to the gunners. The next day the Harbour was attacked again and Malta's fighter aircraft destroyed eleven of the intruders, another eight being eliminated by the guns.

The British Prime Minister was so delighted that he sent the Governor, General Dobbie, a telegram on 21 January 1941:

I send you on behalf of the War Cabinet our heartfelt congratulations upon the magnificent ever-memorable defeat which your heroic garrison and citizens aided by the Navy and above all by the Royal Air Force are making against Italian and German attacks. The eyes of all Britain and indeed of the whole British Empire are watching Malta in her struggle day by day, and we are sure that success as well as glory will reward your efforts.[12]

Two days later General Dobbie replied:

> By God's help Malta will not weaken. We are glad to be able to make a contribution to the victory which we know is sure and certain.[13]

On the same day the *Illustrious,* now repaired, steamed out of Malta for Alexandria. The blitz on this heavily armoured aircraft carrier represented a new era. With the coming of the Luftwaffe the dockyards, the aerodromes and the civilian centres of population had been blasted and shattered by the ever-increasing weight of bombs. Fortunately the principal target, the *Illustrious,* had survived.

In February a new hazard became apparent when parachute mines began to descend from German and Italian aircraft on to the waters on either side of Valletta, some of them exploding in the dockyards. Halfway through the month the air war intensified, when the Luftwaffe attempted to achieve superiority by bringing in Messerschmitt 109s. Their considerable advantage in numbers put great pressure on the Hurricane pilots. Towards the end of the month Luqa was heavily bombed, and at least six Wellington bombers were destroyed.

Slowly, bit by bit, the RAF was losing air supremacy in the face of overwhelming odds, through a process of attrition. The Axis had lost nearly a hundred aircraft over Malta since Italy came into the war and the RAF had lost about sixteen fighters. The difference was that the Axis countries had plenty of spare aircraft and the RAF did not. Even so, some food supplies were getting through and a small convoy reached the island in March, under cover of bad weather. In addition, twelve Mark II Hurricanes were flown to Malta from the *Ark Royal,* in the hope that they would be more than a match for the ME109s.

By this time Rommel's Afrika Korps was operating in North Africa, and it was a source of anxiety that supplies were reaching his men through the port of Tripoli. Accordingly Admiral Cunningham sent four destroyers to

Malta, and on 10 April they came across an Italian convoy of five ships. For the loss of one destroyer, whose crew was saved, five Italian merchantmen and three destroyers were sunk.[14] This made certain that hundreds of tons of vital supplies and ammunition never reached Rommel. Towards the end of April more Hurricanes arrived, and the Wellingtons and Swordfish bombers began to strike back at Rommel's supply lines.

General Dobbie wrote to the Secretary of State for the Colonies on 10 May, describing the Maltese reaction to the bombing:

> This extensive damage to their principal city which was founded immediately after the great Siege in 1565, and has stood unchanged since the time of the knights has been a profound shock to Maltese sentiment and damage to several large churches, including the Cathedral of St John has given deep offence . . . They have been hardened in anger against the enemy, and are facing their own individual calamities with cheerfulness and fortitude. . . As one of them recently said after the destruction of his home "We will endure anything except the rule of these barbarians and savages".[15]

Later on in May it was noticed that there was a relaxation in the bombing. There was of course a reason. The German High Command had been distracted by the withdrawal of the British armed forces to Crete, after Greece had been overwhelmed by the advancing German army. For the time being the German High Command's attention was concentrated on Crete, and not Malta. Field Marshal Keitel and General Jodl favoured an operation against Malta, regarding the island as "the British base of greater strategic importance and danger to us".

Goering resolved that the assault should be on Crete, which he thought would be the easier alternative, and Hitler supported him. The Invasion was ordered, with Goering in command.[16] On 20 May 1941 German parachute divisions invaded Crete, closely supported by the Luftwaffe. The New Zealand, Australian, British and Greek and Cretan soldiers mauled the only German parachute Brigade, but what eventually turned the battle was the fact that the Luftwaffe had complete air superiority. The XI German Air Corps reported "exceptionally high and bloody losses", and Air Fleet IV expressed the view that "absolute air supremacy" should be "the essential condition for the success of any airborne attack".[17]

All this had its relevance for Malta. In order to achieve their costly victory in Crete, the Luftwaffe in Greece was brought up to full strength. Not content with taking Crete, Hitler was thinking in terms of the *Drang Nach Osten*—the Drive to the East. On 22 June Germany invaded the Soviet Union, and some of the Luftwaffe in Sicily were diverted to the Russian front.

At just the moment when Malta's naval base, strike aircraft and Hurricanes were hardest pressed, these developments came as a much needed respite in the fighting. For a time the subjugation of Malta was no longer a top priority to the Axis.

On 2 June General Dobbie, having sent a small detachment of soldiers to Gozo, the small island nearby, wrote to the Chief of the Imperial General Staff that Malta must prepare herself against seaborne and airborne attack. Ending his letter, Dobbie stated his belief that success depended on God, and referred to the Old Testament. The prophet Elisha had been compassed about by enemies and his servant came to him, asking how they would do. Elisha prayed, asking the Lord to open the eyes of his servant and the young man saw that "the mountain was full of horses and chariots of fire round about Elisha". When this letter was passed on, Winston Churchill, realising that General Dobbie placed his ultimate faith in an even higher authority than the Prime Minister, merely initialled the correspondence without comment.[18]

Dobbie told the Maltese in July that Malta would not be given up, and that the garrison had no intention of allowing capture by either the Italians or the Germans. He encouraged them with the words "With God's help we shall succeed". In the meantime in May, July and September 1941, convoys broke through to Malta, and the defence forces took the opportunity to build up a devastating strike force within the Central Mediterranean.

The new Air Officer Commanding, Air Vice Marshal Sir Hugh Lloyd, was an expert on bombing strategy. Along with submarine forces, Wellington and Blenheim bombers would attack convoys by day. Fleet Air Arm Swordfish and Albacores would attack by night. In June more than seventy per cent of the German and Italian ships operating from Italy to North Africa were sunk, many of them by bomber sorties carried out from Malta.

This was a highly effective form of warfare. Every time an oil tanker exploded, the effect was the same as the systematic destruction of hundreds of petrol howsers. Each time a transport ship carrying tanks, guns and ammunition was sunk, weapons disappeared which would have taken hundreds, perhaps even thousands of bombing missions to destroy once deployed in the Western desert.

On Malta the defences were strengthened. The beaches and aerodromes were obstructed with barbed wire entanglements and mines, and more anti-aircraft guns were put in position around the aerodromes as precautions against possible invasion. That summer it seemed that the islanders and the defence forces were experiencing the lull before a storm.

＊　　＊　　＊　　＊　　＊

On 25 July 1941 a very odd episode interrupted the lull. A seaborne force was noticed approaching Malta shortly before midnight, and the sound of motorboat engines was heard. There was an explosion when a torpedo-carrying craft hit the shore fortifications. The searchlights were turned on and illuminated a number of Italian E boats, followed by several other torpedo boats. Immediately the Maltese and British shore gunners opened fire, and within two minutes five E boats were destroyed. Not one achieved the object, which had been to penetrate the harbour.

At first light RAF fighters went into hot pursuit and sank the last four E boats. The Italian Navy had seemingly sent these torpedo boats on a suicidal mission, knowing that the men who volunteered would be killed or become prisoners, even if they caused any damage in the harbour. [19]

Throughout the following months Malta's offensive strikes were intensified, her torpedo-carrying aircraft and submarines threatening Rommel's life-line of supplies to North Africa. In September, October and November, submarines sank or damaged nineteen ships, virtually cutting off supplies to Libya, and Malta-based aircraft flew more than 450 bomber sorties. [20]

The German records later revealed that of 123,000 tons convoyed from Italy to North Africa, in October, November and December 1941, 57,800 tons were sunk, 20,400 were damaged and only 44,800 were delivered. In all, only 36 per cent of the materials and weapons sent to Rommel actually reached him.

The war in the Desert was to a large extent a war of logistics, and the Afrika Korps had been so reduced in strength on account of lack of supplies, that Rommel had to retreat before the British Eighth Army.

One naval action carried out from Malta helped particularly in this process, and will long be remembered in the annals of British Naval History. On 5 November Naval Force K, which included the cruisers *Penelope* and *Aurora,* as well as the destroyers *Lance* and *Lively,* came out from Malta after a photo-reconnaissance report that a large convoy was steaming towards North Africa from Italy.

Force K met the convoy, immediately sank two Italian destroyers and dealt with the merchantmen. They were assisted by the British submarine *Upholder* which sank two more destroyers. The total score for the night was four enemy destroyers sunk, as well as ten large merchant vessels laden with every kind of supply for Rommel. [21]

It was events such as this that caused Count Ciano to write in his Diary that when a convoy sailed, all Italian hearts were in their mouths.[22] But while the Italians soon became demoralised, the Germans, on the other hand, called for vengeance.

Malta held the key to victory in the Mediterranean and had become the most potent British overseas base in the world. As long as Malta's defence forces were striking at the convoys taking tanks, guns and munitions to Rommel, the Afrika Korps would never be secure. But if Malta was eliminated a flood of reinforcements could be shipped across the Mediterranean, so that Egypt, the Suez Canal, and the oil reserves of the Middle East might fall into German hands.

In December 1941 the Luftwaffe returned to Sicily with Field Marshal Kesselring, who had commanded them in the Battle of Britain.[23] This time the Luftwaffe arrived in enormous strength, with more than six hundred of the most modern up-to-date front line aircraft. The siege was about to enter its most deadly phase.

Chapter Two

HITLER, OPERATION HERCULES AND CHURCHILL

FIELD Marshal Kesselring had orders to ensure safe lines of communication with the Afrika Korps in Libya and Cyrenaica, and to "neutralise" Malta. As soon as he arrived in Sicily, the balance of power in the Mediterranean shifted heavily in favour of the Axis.

U Boats sank the aircraft carrier *Ark Royal,* two cruisers and the battleship *Barham.* Kesselring himself sent wave after wave of German bombers to Malta: their bombs shattered the dockyards, the harbour installations, the aerodromes, the centres of communication and the ancient streets and buildings. Valletta was experiencing the same kind of blitz as London and Coventry, except that the bombs were concentrated within a very small area, Greater London being even larger than Malta.

By early December 1941 sixty or seventy Axis aircraft were attacking each week, and later the number grew to not less than two hundred, with pitifully few Hurricanes to oppose them. But still Malta struck back. On 4 January 1942 Blenheim bombers destroyed thirty-five German and Italian bombers lined up at the Sicilian aerodrome Castel Vetrano.[1] Other attacks followed and RAF fighters provided an escort for the convoy steaming towards Malta on 19 January.

After the arrival of the convoy German bombing intensified, and in January and February 1942 there were about two thousand Axis bomber sorties over Malta. As a result the activities of Malta's bombers were greatly reduced in scope, and Axis shipping losses in their convoys to North Africa dropped radically.

In January not a single Axis ship supplying North Africa was sunk. Gradually air superiority was slipping away from the Royal Air Force. Bomb craters were constantly appearing on the runways of the aerodromes and only the work of the Army managed to keep them operational.

The Manchesters and Inniskillings were at Takali, the Devons at Hal Far and the Royal West Kents and the Buffs were at Luqa. Their efforts in removing wrecked aircraft, in filling up the bomb holes, in smoothing and rolling the runways were of supreme importance in keeping the RAF in the air. Much of their repair work was completed at night time, with the help of lamps.[2]

The soldiers of these Regiments built many miles of runway and constructed 170 fighter blast pens, fourteen bomber pens and thirty for the Fleet Air Arm. The Hampshires linked up Luqa and Hal Far by devoloping the Safi strip, a track along which blast pens were established on both sides, amid the rocks and sand, where aircraft could be camouflaged. Next to the blast pens were slit trenches into which the soldiers would go when the Axis bombers arrived, and from which they could and would fire their rifles and Bren guns.

The pilots and soldiers had a special relationship, so dependent were they on each other. The soldiers sent to each blast pen took a special pride whenever their pilot shot down an Axis aircraft, chalking up his victory as if it were their own. And if and when their pilot did not return his loss was their loss.[3]

With bombing day and night, there was little time for sleep. Flight Lieutenant Dickinson and his assistants had to deal with the unexploded bombs.[4] As the bombing increased early in 1942, the work of the defence forces became harder. As soon as aircraft were repaired more were damaged and grounded. Group Captain Woodhall, Malta's outstanding fighter controller, could sometimes only send up four or six fighters to meet massive raids, and the German aircrafts' cannons were superior to the Hurricanes' machine guns. As every day passed Malta's defence forces were becoming more strained.

As yet the full impact of what might happen had not sunk home in Whitehall. On 8 January the Prime Minister had read a Report that an attempt to capture Malta by invasion was improbable until the enemy could judge whether their bombing had neutralised the island.[5]

This picture soon changed. On 27 February the Secretary of State for the Colonies, Lord Cranborne, wrote to the Prime Minister regretting the shortage of supplies in Malta. He ended by saying:

> This is hardly the place to discuss the consequences likely to follow the loss of Malta, not the least of which would be the surrender of 300,000 most loyal British subjects, who would then be verging on starvation, to the mercy of the enemy. . . I feel it my duty to emphasise that unless supplies can be substantially replenished within the next two months, the fortress will be within measurable distance of falling into enemy hands.[6]

He might almost have guessed that two weeks before, on 13 February, the subject of Malta had come to Hitler's attention when Grand Admiral Raeder visited his Headquarters in Berlin. Raeder put forward a plan for the invasion of Malta as a necessary preliminary to the subjugation of North Africa and the Middle East. Hitler agreed and the invasion plan was named Operation Hercules, after the mythical figure who always overcame the superhuman obstacles in his way.

On 29 and 30 April, at Berchtesgaden, Hitler and Mussolini hammered out the details with Marshal Cavallero, the Italian Commander-in-Chief, and General Jodl of the German Armed Forces High Command. Early July was scheduled as the date for the invasion. Mussolini arranged for a battalion of engineers as well as parachute divisions of two regiments to hold themselves in readiness, and Hitler gave orders for two German paratroop battalions to be sent in order to stiffen the Italian assault.

The paratroopers were to land in South East Malta after the island had been bombed with maxium severity, and naval support and ships for transport were to be laid on for the invasion. Preparations for the invasion were now set in hand.[7]

Meanwhile in Malta nearly a thousand tons of bombs were dropped in February and well in excess of two thousand in March, many exploding around the airfields and the submarine base. On 5 March Air Vice-Marshal Lloyd sent a signal to his Commander-in-Chief that Malta most urgently needed Spitfires.[8] His request was granted and on 7 March the first Spitfires bound for Malta took off from HMS *Eagle* near Gibraltar. They were immediately in action against the Messerschmitt 109s, while the Hurricanes with their lesser armament were sent to deal with the Axis bombers.

One of the Gunners manning the anti-aircraft batteries, Major Gilchrist, wrote in admiration:

Spitfires began to make a welcome appearance in the air, but they were hopelessly outnumbered by the enemy fighters. Perhaps the most heroic sight throughout a heroic year was to see about half a dozen of these fighters in the air, taking on all comers. They were frequently shot down, but seldom without first having scored a success against their opponents.[9]

The fighter pilots were not the only ones to be hard-pressed. That same month Malta experienced a grave disappointment. The February convoy had failed to arrive and the next convoy from Alexandria ran into trouble in March. An Italian battle fleet of one battleship, six cruisers and a host of destroyers intercepted a much smaller British naval force, consisting of some five light cruisers. By use of smoke-screens the British Navy fought a brilliant defensive action, drawing off the Italians, who did not continue fighting after nightfall. This engagement had an important psychological effect on the Germans. Although the Italian Navy was strong, the Germans henceforth relied not on the Italian Navy but on the Luftwaffe and on U Boat warfare.[10]

Meanwhile on 23 March one of the four merchant ships in the convoy, the *Breconshire,* carrying oil, was sunk by bombs just outside Malta's Grand Harbour. Another, *Glen Campbell,* went down a few minutes later. Only two ships the *Pampas* and the *Talabot*, made harbour, where they were bombed on 26 March. The *Pampas* caught fire and sank, and the *Talabot* was hit; only part of their cargo was saved. Having eluded the Italian Navy, the March convoy had almost completely failed because of the activities of the Luftwaffe.[11]

Now that the German bombers were coming to Malta with such large numbers of fighters to protect them, the Spitfires were switched into action against them, for the time being leaving the ME109s. Above all, more Spitfires were required, and in the form of squadrons. The calls for urgent assistance for Malta were taken up at a very senior level in the Air Ministry, and on 27 March Group Captain Bouchier, DFC, Deputy Director of Fighter Operations, put in writing the case for sending active Squadrons of Spitfires to Malta.

> Our fighter pilots place no great premium on life. Their greatest desire is to fight on and with their Squadron or Wing for as long as they can. Esprit de corps is terrific. Their confidence in themselves and their Squadrons is born of good team work and flying together. Fighter Squadron pilots do not only fly together, they play together, drink together, eat together, talk together. They become very attached to each other and their leaders. It is a greater sadness to them than most people appreciate to be constantly uprooted in penny numbers from what to them is everything on earth—their Squadron and their friends.[12]

As Bouchier penned these thoughts the Maltese population and defence forces were gradually being starved. On 29 March the Chiefs of Staff made a representation to Winston Churchill. They suggested that a message from the King might be a source of encouragement, at a time when the islanders were suffering such fierce attacks, accompanied by disappointment at the loss of the much-needed stores from the convoy. Within twenty-four hours King George VI had sent a telegram:

> I have been watching with admiration the stout-hearted resistance of all in Malta. . . to the fierce and constant air attacks of the enemy in recent weeks. In the active defence of the island the Royal Air Force have been ably supported by the Royal Malta Artillery, and it therefore gives me special pleasure in recognition of their skill and resolution to assume the Colonelcy-in-Chief of the Regiment.[13]

This telegram arrived at a time when the Governor feared that Malta might go under. On 1 April General Dobbie signalled to the War Office: "It is obvious that the very worst must happen if we cannot replenish our vital needs". Wheat and flour, fodder, oils, coal and ammunition were most urgently needed. The bread ration for the Maltese was not more than ten-and-a-half ounces a day, and many necessities, such as sugar, were in extremely short supply. The victory kitchens issued a hot meal to the Maltese every day, but this did not amount to more than the barest minimum. Starvation and invasion seemed only a few weeks away.[14]

The bombing had taken a terrible toll. The tons of bombs dropped on Malta in March and April 1942 exceeded the number of bombs which had hurtled down on London in the whole of 1940. Over ten thousand houses had been reduced to debris, with rubble blocking the roads, and more than twenty thousand other houses were badly damaged. Even a hundred churches has been wrecked or destroyed, as if the Germans and the Italians, who had brought the Germans, wished to show their contempt for the work of the Knights of Malta, who had fought as Crusaders so many centuries before.

By April well over a thousand civilians had lost their lives through the indiscriminate bombing, and many of the Maltese population were living almost permanently in the underground shelters or in the catacombs. They often had to queue for water for long periods after the "All Clear" had sounded. For the Maltese the war had become one for existence.

The deficiency of the daily diet began to lead to disease, and the Governor, General Dobbie, for all his strength and resolve, warned that if the total population of 270,000 began to go under on account of starvation, Malta would fall. He had done a great deal to strengthen Malta's defences by constructing shore fortifications and by building and developing the underground tunnels and centres. But the haunted expressions of starving women and children weighed on his mind.[15]

Miss Mabel Strickland, Editor of *The Times of Malta* sent Lord Louis Mountbatten a telegram on 21 April, implying that General Dobbie's removal was "vitally essential and urgent", her reason being that there was a lack of co-ordination between the Armed Services. This was reported to the Prime Minister under the heading "The Strickland Intrigue". The War Cabinet was informed, and invited the Minister of State to travel to the Middle East, and to report whether in his view a change of Governor should be made.

When the Report came back, the Chiefs of Staff from the Middle East Defence Committee and the three Services Commanders in Malta confirmed that General Dobbie was tired, had lost grip of the situation, and was no longer capable of affording the higher direction and control vital in the circumstances. The Minister, Walter Monckton, who knew General Dobbie to be a person of courage and high character most reluctantly came to the same conclusion. Accordingly Churchill and the War Cabinet agreed that Dobbie should be replaced, and that the new Governor should be General Lord Gort VC.[16]

Churchill told Lord Gort that they regarded him as the man to render "this vitally important service",[17] and he, Winston Churchill, would do everything in his power to make certain that a convoy of supplies would reach Malta in the latter part of June. He made it clear that the Governor General Dobbie had performed with great courage and deserved a rest.

Churchill took steps to ensure that the new Governor would also act as Commander-in-Chief and Supreme

Commander in Malta. He informed Dominion Prime Ministers that Lord Gort had been ordered to prolong the resistance of the fortress to the utmost limit, and that the War Cabinet regarded him as the man to save the fortress. [18]

Like General Dobbie, the Fighter Pilots had been under great pressure. They were continually in action and it was not unusual for four or six Spitfires to be confronted by eighty German bombers with a large Fighter Escort of Messerschmitt 109s above them waiting to attack. The aerodromes were bombed about four times a day, and the fighting was so intense that orders were in force for compulsory rest periods after three months, to give relief to exhausted pilots no longer at the peak of physical condition. It was when pilots were very tired that they were most likely to be shot down.

The situation was critical. Churchill knew that the Maltese and the British in Malta were starving, and he had already been told by the Polish leader, General Sikorski, that Hitler planned to invade Malta. [19] Churchill's reaction was one of total defiance.

He resolved that Malta must be fed with Spitfires; the only question was how to get them there? The Aircraft Carrier *Argus* was not available and the *Eagle,* which had been loosing off packets of a few Spitfires some six hundred miles west of Malta, was having its steering gear repaired. This would last at least a month, and extremely urgent action was required. [20]

The six hundred or more German and Italian fighters and bombers in Sicily were now faced by a mere twenty or thirty serviceable British fighter aircraft in Malta. If these fighters were destroyed the Island Fortress would not be able to withstand a large invasion force with overwhelming Luftwaffe support. Moreover the British Commonwealth Forces would be unable to prevent tanks, artillery and aircraft reinforcing Rommel's Afrika Korps in North Africa. If that happened the opportunity to resume a successful offensive against Rommel with all possible speed would be finished for a long time to come.

On 1 April Winston Churchill outlined these facts to

President Roosevelt of the USA in a strong personal appeal for help. He received an answer by return: the President had not been found wanting.[21]

King George VI also had been thinking about Malta. He wished to do something more than send a telegram. On his own personal initiative he resolved to give Malta and the Maltese people an honour which had never before been awarded to any country in the British Empire and Commonwealth: the George Cross. On 15 April 1942 Sir William Dobbie received this message from the King:

> To honour her brave people I award the George Cross to the Island Fortress of Malta: to bear witness to a heroism and devotion that will long be famous in History.[22]

General Dobbie replied on behalf of the people and garrison of Malta:

> By God's help Malta will not weaken, but will endure until victory is won.[23]

The Times of Malta announced the news under the headline: "King Sets His Seal on Living History".

On the same day in Malta, a Spitfire pilot, Johnny Johnston, DFC, who had shot down five or six German aircraft, was writing up his Diary. He had recently been reading about the great siege of Malta in 1565, when the 641 Knights of St John with the Maltese garrison under la Valette, Grand Master of the Knights, had fought off more than 30,000 Turkish invaders.

Johnston recalled that after his arrival in Malta his Commanding Officer had said that they would keep fighting as long as there was a single serviceable aircraft. He found himself wondering whether he really could keep fighting to the finish. On the whole he thought that he could, but he was not certain. That night he recorded in his Diary an extraordinary rumour.

> The latest Maltese story is that a convoy of three

American aircraft carriers is bringing not less than 150 Spits to the island; that's the silliest one we've yet heard. These rumours play on alarm and despondency . . . they're probably the work of Fifth Columnists.[24]

Some days earlier in Britain, unknown to Johnny Johnston, the Spitfire Squadron Commander of 603 (City of Edinburgh) Squadron Lord David Douglas-Hamilton had received a call at the Officers' Mess at Dyce Airport, Aberdeen, from his Flight Commander John Buckstone. The message was so secret that it could not be passed over the telephone. Buckstone hurried to see him, saying that the Squadron was being posted to the Middle East. He added that he had seen reports from Malta of the numbers of aircraft shattered by bombs, and it looked as if Malta had had it.[25]

On 12 April the Squadron was taken by bus to Port Glasgow, where before them lay a huge American aircraft carrier, the USS *Wasp,* with Spitfires being hoisted on to the flight deck. At 8.30p.m., along with pilots from 601 (County of London) Squadron, the pilots of 603 Squadron began to board.

Although David Douglas-Hamilton commanded the Edinburgh Squadron only he and his second in command, Bill Douglas, were Scots, the other pilots coming from the USA, Canada, New Zealand, South Africa, Belgium, Ireland, and England. Many of them had never fired their guns in anger.

Young and inexperienced as the Spitfire pilots may have been, they were "an all-important"[26] part of Winston Churchill's personal response to Hitler's plans for the invasion of Malta. Not only that, they were going with the blessing and goodwill of President Roosevelt of the USA.

As David Douglas-Hamilton looked at the USS *Wasp* he resolved that wherever they might be going, with Bill Douglas he would keep a record of the activities of their Squadron. The Squadron Diary which they wrote covers the central part of the Malta story.

Part II

"In the future, after this war, when the name of Malta is mentioned, you will be able to say with pride, 'I was there'."

Air Vice Marshall Sir Hugh Pughe Lloyd
to the Spitfire Pilots
20 April 1942.

Chapter Three
THE SQUADRON COMMANDER AND HIS DIARY.

DAVID Douglas-Hamilton was the youngest of a family of four brothers unique in the Royal Air Force. All four were professional flying instructors, and all later became Squadron Commanders.

David had been to St Andrews University and to Balliol College, Oxford, where he had been Captain of the University Boxing team, winning most of his fights by knock-out, from a height of 6 feet 4 inches. His eldest brother, Douglas, had been Scottish Middleweight Boxing Champion, and in 1933, while serving as an MP, had become the first pilot to fly over Mount Everest. David also had a passion for flying, and learned to do so with the Oxford University Air Squadron.

By 1935 Douglas was commanding 602 (City of Glasgow) Auxiliary Air Force Bomber Squadron; David's next brother, Geordie, commanded 603 (City of Edinburgh) Auxiliary Air Force Fighter Squadron, and his third brother, Malcolm, had entered the RAF through Cranwell, where he trained with Douglas Bader. David chose to gain his flying experience in a Tiger Moth with his brother Malcolm.

Contrary to his expectations, Britain did not go to War during the Munich crisis of 1938 but he was certain War was coming. The time for commitment had arrived and he joined the Auxiliary Air Force. On 15 October he married Prunella Stack, the leader of the Women's League of Health and Beauty. He never concealed from her the fact that he longed to become a fighter pilot.

After the outbreak of War David was sent to Hastings, where pilots of Volunteer Reserve Units were drafted for further training. To his irritation he learnt that all his years of flying counted little with the RAF. He would have to complete exhaustive training courses before becoming a flying instructor.

His other brothers were involved elsewhere. Douglas, who was a Controller with 11 Group, was sent to France on 17 May 1940, by Air Chief Marshal Dowding, in order to make contact with all the Fighter Squadrons operating there. This he did, flying in a Magister, for which he received a mention in Despatches. He found that the Germans were pouring through the French defences, and that there was chaos everywhere. When he reported back, Dowding made it clear that this information confirmed the correctness of his resolve to preserve the bulk of Fighter Command for the defence of the United Kingdom.[1]

Meanwhile, David's brother, Geordie, had become Chief Intelligence Officer of Fighter Command at the Headquarters at Bentley Priory, where he worked closely with the Commander-in-Chief. The third brother, Malcolm, was training the Greek Air Force pilots in Salisbury, Rhodesia, and David wrote to him that he was "pulling all possible strings to get to Fighters".[2]

To his bitter disappointment, however, he was posted not to Fighters but to Netheravon as an Instructor, with the acting rank of Flight Lieutenant. One of his friends in the RAF, whom he had met while training at Hastings, was Richard Hillary, who belonged to 603 (City of Edinburgh) Squadron, and whose book *The Last Enemy* became one of the best accounts of life as a Battle of Britain pilot.

David had hoped more than he could say that he would be able to take his place as a Battle of Britain pilot, but was told that he was required as an Instructor at Netheravon. All he could do to break the monotony was to lay on bouts of Exhibition Boxing with the former English Heavyweight Boxing Champion, Freddie Mills. The months ticked away until suddenly, in the summer of 1941, David received news which filled him with excitement. He was to be posted to a Fighter Operational Training Unit: soon he joined 603 Squadron.

David's first Operational Mission took place on 27 November when he and other pilots attacked German flak ships in the North Sea off Germany. His letter to his wife, giving all the details, was written with the fulfilment of a man who felt that at last he was being given the opportunity to serve his country.

Great news today. I have been under fire for the first time! You may have heard in the News tonight that "our fighters" and Hurry-bombers sank a supply ship and two flak ships. Well, we did the two flak ships, and I did my bit to help one of them go down.

Nobody was lost at all, not even hit, although we saw flak bursting all round and red streaks coming up at us. Three of us all attacked the same flak-ship and criss-crossed it with cannon-fire. The merchant ship went up in a huge cloud of white smoke after a bomb hit it—it must have burst its boilers. A terrific sight!

We had to go over seventy miles of "Drink" to get there, and I must say it seemed an awfully long way, but I never felt frightened the whole way, least of all during the action. You can guess I am happy to have had a crack at them at last, and to have been able to fire in earnest.[3]

The Operations Record Book of 603 Squadron contained a mention of the telegram sent by the Air Officer Commanding 11 Group of congratulation on a fine performance in sinking the two flak ships and the supply ship.[4] But these attacks did not always work out as happily, and the tone of the next letter was very different. His sortie on 8 December over France ran into trouble at Le Touquet, and this time everything went wrong from the start.

We were escorting some bombers about twenty miles into France and were flying at about 20,000 feet. We dived as we crossed the coast, and soon thereafter the 109s attacked us out of the sun.

We turned left and they were all in among us—I got my first close-up glimpse of 109s and Focke-Wulf 190s with their black crosses. More and more of them were

51

coming in, until we must have had about twenty of them against us.

I fired my first burst literally about a mile out of range—but it was excusable as it was my first. Then I began to realise that I was not merely the spectator of a dog-fight, but was being given some opportunities to shoot the blighters down.

So I fired at two more crossing my bows; one very close at about twenty-five yards, but I fear I hit nothing as I did not allow enough for deflection. Then I was on the tail of one and fired till my cannon gave out, and I only had machine guns left.

Then we were going North up the French coast, when I saw more coming down on me, so turned sharp left and blacked right out; but when I had got right round, the Squadron were too far ahead, so I dived straight down to sea-level with throttle and everything wide open doing 400 plus mph.

I was belting along over the sea when all of sudden the aeroplane was thrown like a leaf up fifty feet, bumping my head on the roof. One minute my maps were in their case, and then fell down to the most inaccessible parts of the cockpit, so I had to return mapless.

I thought at first "How funny that there should be such bumps over the sea", and then I remembered about Flak.

I again did not feel very worried during the action . . . I am quite certain that if it had not been so new to me, I could have got some of those Huns. However, I shall do better next time.

So there it all is—I would have thoroughly enjoyed the whole show if it had not been for our losses.[5]

The Operation Record Book for that day confirmed that Flying Officer Fawkes, Pilot Officer Falconer and Sergeant Bennett were missing after the surprise attack over Le Touquet. Flight Lieutenant Douglas-Hamilton and others had fired at enemy aircraft, without success that could be observed.[6]

He was now a keen member of 603 City of Edinburgh Squadron whose motto was "Gin Ye Daur" ("If You Dare"). In 1939, just before the war and just after his brother Geordie had commanded the Squadron, 603 had received an award as the best squadron in the Auxiliary Air Force. But since that time all of its experienced Battle of Britain pilots had been posted elsewhere, and the turnover of pilots had been very rapid.

On 18 December 1941 David's Commanding Officer, Squadron Leader Forshaw, was lost in action. He had been scrambled to intercept an enemy aircraft over the North Sea, and had not returned. A few weeks earlier Forshaw had kindly turned a blind eye when David, contrary to all the rules, had flown his wife Prunella in a Spitfire. The Squadron Leader had been a generous Commanding Officer.

David was asked to take command of the Squadron and they trained at Dyce, near Aberdeen. On 19 February, according to the Operation Record Book, "some formation flying took place, with some authorised low flying, the whole being an impressive sight, and said much for the leadership of the CO, Squadron Leader Douglas-Hamilton".[7]

The first thirteen days of March were spent on Convoy patrols and training, and on 14 March the Squadron moved to Peterhead, engaged in training exercises with units of the 51st Highland Division. At the end of the month members of the Squadron received their first inkling that they might be sent abroad, when they were ordered to arrive at Port Glasgow on 12 April. There they were met by twelve other pilots who had been posted to join them.

As he looked at the aircraft carrier, the USS *Wasp*, David noticed and mentioned in the Squadron Diary that nine of the pilots, including Tony Holland, had never flown on offensive sorties.

When this news reached the Air Ministry, furious notes flew around to the effect that Malta was no place for inexperienced pilots, who might be the first to be shot down, but it was too late to have second thoughts.[8] By

10a.m. on 13 April the *Wasp,* carrying forty-seven Spitfires, had left Port Glasgow, slightly damaging its screw on the mudbank. At 6a.m. on the 14th she was moving slowly down the Irish Sea, escorted by the Royal Navy's Battle Cruiser HMS *Renown* and six British destroyers.[9]

It was only then that it dawned on the pilots that they would be soon flying their Spitfires off the carrier in some unknown sea. None of 603's pilots had done this before.

David's two Flight Commanders, who had boarded with him, were Bill Douglas and John Buckstone. Douglas, who commanded A Flight had completed his training in 1940, and had begun operational flying that year. He had shot down an ME109 and damaged at least one other, before being wounded over France. This had stopped him flying for several months. Buckstone, who commanded B flight, had been in a ground job early on in the War, but had volunteered for flying, and had completed some sweeps over France. He had been married a few weeks before.

The other pilots came from all over the world. The one David had known for longest was the Irishman Neville King, who was his wife's first cousin. King had been a London policeman, defusing unexploded German bombs during the London Blitz, and he considered that the best way he could serve the Allied Cause would be to become a Spitfire pilot.

The pilots soon settled down and found that they were billeted in cabins, sometimes sharing with American officers. One of them was slightly taken aback to be sharing with a Dr. Messersmith. It soon became evident that when a senior American officer addressed a Squadron Leader as "Sir" this was a formality, and where the RAF would use the word "Sir" the American sailors would say "Okay Chief!"

In all respects the hospitality shown to the pilots by the American officers and men was of the higest standard. The food was excellent, with a variety of drinks including coffee, tea, and chocolate, and it was a considerable thrill for the pilots to be able to eat two eggs for breakfast. The only surprise was that the *Wasp*, like all American naval ships, was teetotal. Indeed the sight of fifty RAF officers and sergeants drinking Coca Cola and fruit drinks in the Wardroom was a memorable one.

On the Hangar Deck the forty-seven Spitfires occupied the entire floor and part of the ceiling. Each had four cannon, a Merlin 46 engine and long-range petrol tanks, hanging under them. On the Flight deck were the US Navy's nineteen Grumman Martlets of the Fighting 71st.

On 15 April, as they watched the coast of Ireland fade into the distance, the pilots were assembled for a talk. They were briefed by Wing Commander Maclean, who told them that they were to be taken some way into the Mediterranean, just North of Algiers. There, out of range of the Luftwaffe, the Spitfires would be flown off the Flight Deck to Malta, keeping close to the African coast. Two much smaller groups of Spitfires making up 249 Squadron, had been flown off HMS *Eagle* on 7 and 31 March, but the forty-seven aeroplanes on the *Wasp* would be far and away the largest reinforcement of Spitfires to be flown to Malta.

Squadron Leader Jumbo Gracie was the only pilot who had flown off the *Eagle* with the earlier Spitfires. He had returned to put the case for Malta's reinforcement in Whitehall, and was able to tell the pilots what it would be like to fly Spitfires with the additional weight of extra fuel tanks and four cannon. The picture he gave of Malta was a very tough one. At the time of his departure there had only been three serviceable Spitfires left. Every day in March about six Spitfires had been sent into action against 150 German bombers, while Malta was "blitzed almost incessantly, and with ever-increasing ferocity".

Gracie had at one time said that he joined the RAF because he liked to do his fighting sitting down, but he was known to be a very efficient officer, and to have shot down eight German aircraft, seven of them bombers. Many of the pilots thought that he must be exaggerating the difficulties in Malta. Even so his words gave rise to panic-buying of razor blades, shoes, underwear, soap, tobacco, and cigarettes from the well-stocked stores, in case there were no more in Malta.

During the afternoon of the next day, the 16 April, the pilots watched excitedly as destroyers manoeuvred in small circles, dropping depth charges on a suspected U-Boat. The next two days consisted in the main of life-boat drill.

At 3a.m. on Sunday 19 April, the *Wasp* passed through the Straits of Gibraltar, meeting as she did so two more cruisers and two more destroyers, giving her the protection of a battle cruiser, two other cruisers and eight destroyers. The British Navy was taking no chances.[10]

＊　　＊　　＊　　＊　　＊

Dr George Borg later recalled that on the same day, as an eighteen-year old, he was crossing the Marsa Wharf with his father and their pony and cart, when they saw German Stukas diving down on the dockyard in Valletta, a few hundred yards away. His father told him to make for the abattoir air-raid shelter. When they arrived they tethered the pony to the gate. It was then that George heard the whistle of a bomb coming down. He hurled himself on the ground, feeling his father's body on top of him. He heard a loud crack and saw a flash, smoke and dust everywhere, rubble and stones weighing down on him, almost as though he was to be buried alive. His clothes had been wrenched off him by the blast, and he was bleeding about his legs and arms.

When the dust began to settle, George saw that where the pony and cart had been, there was now "only a large ugly hole". His father way lying twelve yards away, unable to stand. George became very agitated and shouted for help. He was pulled down into the shelter, while the bombing continued, and then he went up with assistance, finding his father covered in blood. All his father would say was, "George, I am dying; I am dying. I did my best to save you." They were taken to the hospital for casualties, the journey taking an hour. By the time they arrived his father was no longer able to speak, and he died soon afterwards.[11]

＊　　＊　　＊　　＊　　＊

Meanwhile, as the Maltese counted their dying and their dead, the USS *Wasp*, with Malta's Relief Force of forty-seven Spitfires ready to take on Kesselring's six hundred aircraft, was moving towards Algiers, less than a thousand miles away. Twelve Spitfires had been moved up to the Flight Deck early on. The next morning they would all have to be flown off, in four groups, led by Squadron Leaders Jumbo Gracie, John Bisdee, David Douglas-Hamilton, and Flight Lieutenant Bill Douglas.

That day the sun was brilliant, reflecting off the deep blue white-crested waves of the Mediterranean. The pilots packed their Spitfires with their personal kit, and prepared their maps for the flight. The engines of the Spitfires were run up, and the long-range tanks, many of which had leaked, were repaired.

One of the pilots of 601 Squadron, Denis Barnham, found himself thinking that the carrier was so steady and peaceful, and the sea in the dazzling sunlight was so wonderful to look upon, it was almost impossible to believe that what lay beyond the horizon was death and blood and dust and destruction.[12]

Chapter Four

THE FIRST USS WASP

MALTA RELIEF FORCE

AT 4.15 a.m. on 20 April, the Spitfire pilots had breakfast on the USS *Wasp*, which lay about thirty-five miles North of Algiers. At 4.45 a.m. they received a final briefing from Wing Commander Maclean.

At 5.30, with dawn spreading across the sky, the Grumman Martlet Wildcat fighters flown by the American pilots took off, clearing the Flight Deck. Then the Spitfires started up their engines. This was a dangerous process in a confined space, and an American who walked into a prop was killed.

At 5.45 the first group of Supermarine Spitfire MkV fighters took off, led by Jumbo Gracie. The tail of one Spitfire went up during take-off, and the aeroplane disappeared over the end of the deck. To everyone's relief, what seemed minutes later, it was seen climbing up towards the sky.

Gracie nearly made a mistake by flying towards Gibraltar instead of Malta, but he was called up on the radio, and quickly corrected his course. David Douglas-Hamilton could not help thinking that if the situation was not so urgent, those in Gibraltar would almost have taken a malicious delight in hearing his explanation as to why his Squadron of Spitfires, setting out for Malta, had landed in Gibraltar.

David was soon to be embarrassed himself. All went well when it came to his turn. His aircraft was pushed on to the left, and as soon as it was on the Flight Deck he started up the engine. He let the brakes off with a snap, and the aircraft slowly gathered speed, becoming airborne just before the end of the deck. After reaching the rendezvous height the other Spitfires formed up behind him and Bill Douglas, with one notable exception.

To David's anger one of the three American pilots in

the Squadron, instead of following, flew his Spitfire in the opposite direction for Algeria. Sergeant Walcott had been with the Edinburgh Squadron for just a month. He belly-landed his Spitfire on the south side of the Atlas Mountains, and went to the nearest US Consul, claiming to be a lost Civil Aviation pilot in need of repatriation. The thought that death might await him in Malta, had preyed on his mind, and he had chosen to desert in the face of the enemy.[1]

What was remarkable was not that one man could not go through with it, but that every other pilot was resolved to accomplish his mission. David himself set course to the East with his Squadron, gaining height. They flew towards the sun, still low on the horizon, with blue sky above and the grey Mediterranean beneath. Through the early morning haze the French African coast could be seen on the right. They were flying at under 200 mph to save petrol.

The weather was ideal, and they never lost sight of the African coast. When they rounded the first corner near Tunis, the Italian island of Pantelleria, which was a base for Luftwaffe fighters, came into sight. As they had been ordered to reinforce Malta and to avoid fighting on the way, the pilots gave Pantelleria a wide berth and at the distance of 100 miles, Malta came into view, with Sicily and Mount Etna also in sight. Malta seemed very small, and the Spitfires started their descent.

Over the radio David heard the Controller in Malta giving instructions to Squadron Leader Gracie, and to a section of Spitfires covering their approach to the island. He learnt that there were ME109s around, but this time he did not see them.

He crossed the coast over a high cliff, not long after the last bombing raid, leading his group towards Takali. On the ground Johnny Johnston, who had earlier heard the Maltese rumour that they would be reinforced, saw the approaching Spitfires and later noted in his Diary: "Always find sight and sound of a large formation is affecting, but this was so welcome and unexpected that it made us all absurdly excited."[2]

The London Squadron flew to Luqa, and David with his Squadron circled Takali and, not noticing the landing-run, completed a formation landing into the wind in sections of four across the runway. Some of the Spitfires stopped within feet of bomb craters. So far none of them had been damaged.

David taxied his Spitfire into one of the blast pens dispersed around Takali and jumped out. He could see Malta's small, yellow-coloured, square houses, and fields honeycombed with stone walls, surrounding fig bushes, green crops and prickly pear. Apart from obvious bomb damage all around, Malta appeared relatively peaceful, at least for the next few minutes.

After David had unpacked his baggage, the ground crew began to refuel his Spitfire and make it ready for battle. A pilot from 249 Squadron was coming down to fly it. As David waited for transport a group of Maltese labourers passed. Pointing to his Spitfire they grinned, giving the thumbs up sign, saying "All right". Perhaps it was the only English they knew, but it expressed the hopes they had that the new Spitfire pilots would relieve Malta from the weight of the bombs they had been experiencing.

The pilots were taken to the Officers' Mess in a rickety bus with worn-out tyres, few windows, and a broken exhaust. Inside, the bus was adorned with many ecclesiastical prints and postcards of the Virgin Mary and child, leaving the fighter pilots in no doubt as to the fervent faith of the Maltese.

Meanwhile the Station Commander, Wing Commander Jack Satchell, DFC, arrived in a car and drove David round the aerodrome, showing him a bomb hole which could have swallowed up a house. There were parts of burnt-out aircraft—Spitfires, Hurricanes, Beaufighters, Marylands and a few Junkers 88s or ME109s—which had been shot down near the aerodrome. Everywhere there were bomb holes, wreckage and battered buildings. Satchell had been bombed out of no less than three buildings, and he used a tent as his Headquarters, his staff being installed underground.

They drove up to the Officers' Mess in the old capital of M'Dina on a small hill overlooking Takali, one mile from the aerodrome. There they learnt that the presence of the new Spitfires had not been unnoticed by the Germans. It was nearly lunchtime when the air-raid siren went, giving warning of the second raid of the day. David and the pilots were told it would take fifteen minutes for the bombers to arrive. They put on their tin hats and went onto the Mess verandah to watch.

David heard the bang of an anti-aircraft gun, then one or two more, these being "pointer" rounds, which by bursting near enemy aircraft, would indicate their position to the six Spitfire and six Hurricane pilots who had been scrambled to intercept them. Takali was bombed. This was how it appeared to David.

We saw the ME109s clearly, weaving in and out of the shell-bursts. Suddenly, gun after gun burst into life, until a first-class barrage was in full swing. The bombers were arriving. The sky rapidly became dotted with shell-bursts, and then we saw them: three, five, ten about twenty JU88s in straggling formation, all making for Takali—our aerodrome. One after another they dived down towards the aerodrome and dispersal areas. We could clearly see them releasing their bombs, and followed the bombs in their flight to earth.

The 88s dived down to about a thousand feet above the ground, and we saw the great explosions of the bombs on their target. Seconds later we heard the noise of the explosions following on the sinister whistle of the falling bombs, and felt the blast. Meanwhile the Bofors guns joined in the din as the 88s came low, shooting up streams of glowing red "cricket-balls" at them. Huge fountains of dust rose up from the aerodrome where the bombs had burst, and in two places there was a thick column of black smoke billowing up. These were obviously petrol fires—they had got two of our nice new Spitfires.

Someone shouted, "The Spits are getting into them!" We looked, and saw three or four Spitfires chasing the

88s. One of them opened fire, and we saw the puffs of smoke from its cannons. Almost at once one of the 88s engines streamed smoke. We lost sight of it, but heard afterwards that it came down in the sea. Then the ME109s got mixed up with the Spitfires, and a general dog-fight ensued.

We were all shouting as if at a football match: "Good show; now you've got him! Look out Spit, 109 coming down on you; turn, man, for God's sake, turn!" Then, "Thank God for that!" as the Spitfire turned and avoided the 109's fire.

The Huns had no sooner finished with Takali than we saw a similar bunch of bombers going for Luqa aerodrome, another for Hal Far aerodrome, and yet another for the Grand Harbour. The harbour party was reinforced with a good sprinkling of JU87s, which amazed us by the steepness of their diving angle. We saw with horror many of the bombs going wide of their mark and bursting among civilian houses and villages.

All this time the entire air over the island was filled with whirling aircraft and anti-aircraft bursts, and the noise of guns, shells, and bombs was intermingled with the rattle of aircraft cannon-fire and the whine of diving aeroplanes. Here and there we saw an 88 streaming smoke, but we never actually saw one crash that day, though it is known that several were destroyed.

For us new arrivals the sight of a first-class bombing raid from a ringside seat was the most staggering thing we had ever experienced. Many of us, including myself, had never even heard the whistle of a bomb before. Some of us had not till now even seen any enemy aircraft, and few of us had seen them in such large numbers, or been able, unmolested, to watch aerial combats from the ground.

It all seemed an incredible spectacle to us coming from comparatively peaceful Britain, and we could hardly believe we were really there. It was more like being at a cinema show, for in many ways one felt quite detached. But now we rapidly learnt to distinguish between the sharp "bang" of an AA gun and the reverberating "woomph" of a bomb. The same performance was repeated again at tea-time, and at dusk we had a fourth raid on Takali.[3]

The Air Officer Commanding, Air Marshal Lloyd, came to Takali with Group Captain Woodhall, the Sector Commander. The latter was one of the most exceptional fighter controllers of the War and he had masterminded countless aerial battles from the ground. Air Marshal Lloyd carefully watched the bombing raids, and counted about twenty-five Junkers 87s and sixty-four Junkers 88s in wave after wave, dive-bombing the small aerodrome. By the end of the day about three hundred Axis bombers had been sent to Malta, mainly to destroy the new Spitfires, many of which were still being serviced before being put back into the air. Forty tons of bombs had been dropped on Luqa immediately, and within three days five hundred tons of bombs were dropped on the Takali and Luqa aerodromes.[4]

Just after 1 p.m. a few pilots were scrambled, including Laddie Lucas and Raoul Daddo-Langlois of 249 Squadron, and on that day the latter showed just how rugged some of the pilots had become. Daddo-Langlois saw an ME109 and attacked it with his Spitfire head-on. Neither of them broke, and the two aircraft collided in mid-air, breaking off the wing of the ME109 and leaving the Spitfire without its wing-tip.

As Daddo-Langlois came into land, a cluster of ME109s tried to machine-gun him, while Hurricanes tried to hold them off. Eventually he landed but overshot, and he pulled up his undercarriage so that the Spitfire skidded to a halt on its belly. He leapt out of the aircraft with machine-gun bullets ploughing up the ground around him, and ran to safety.

Episodes like this made the Spitfire pilots sure that on equal terms their aeroplanes were more than a match for the ME109s. But not all pilots were as lucky as Daddo-Langlois.[5]

At 5.20 p.m. that day Johnny Johnston was scrambled with four other pilots. Some minutes later, as Luqa was being bombed, he saw two ME109s diving down through the smoke to shoot up the aerodrome, so he made for them and flew straight into the explosion of a very large bomb. The aircraft was thrown up into the air, climbing steeply and banking at sixty degrees, out of control. He struggled out of his helmet and oxygen mask, pushed the stick forward, shot half out of the cockpit, his parachute catching and holding him back. Throwing back his head and shoulders as hard as he could, he somersaulted backwards into the air, and his parachute opened 150 feet above the ground. His Spitfire crashed in flames, the ammunition going off in the heat. Johnston was helped back to the Officers' Mess to learn that two of the other Spitfire pilots who had taken off had not returned.[6]

Air Marshal Lloyd noticed the reaction of the new pilots to all this, and wrote: "There had never been such an exhibition of concentrated bombing. The newly arrived pilots were speechless. They had never seen anything like it."[7] That evening Lloyd and Woodhall addressed the new pilots, putting them in the picture about what had happened, and what would be expected of them. It is of interest to read the vivid impression they made on David at this time: "There is no doubt that those two men, who with dogged tenacity ran the aerial defence of the island during its most difficult period, have earned the undying gratitude of Malta."

Air Vice-Marshal Lloyd made a point of arriving just when a heavy blitz was about to begin, much to the anxiety of his Headquarters staff. Disdaining shelters, he toured the dispersal areas with bombs bursting all round his car.

Group Captain Woodhall also was absolutely tireless, and always considered the pilots first. During practically every big raid on the island from February he controlled the fighters from the operating room. It was a miracle how he stood up to the strain, but every pilot was extremely grateful that he did; for nothing was better calculated to inspire confidence during a big battle than "Woody" giving instructions on the R/T in his calm, friendly voice.

The AOC finished his talk to us with the words: "In the future, after this war, when the name of Malta is mentioned, you will be able to say with pride, 'I was there!' " At that moment the whole building shook with the crash of the bombs of the dusk raid.

Ever after that, whenever anyone went through some particularly trying experience, such as a near miss by a bomb, or being shot up in the air, he would be chaffed with the words: "Never mind, you'll still be able to say 'I Was There!' ".

After Woodhall's talk urging the pilots to strike back as hard as possible at the Luftwaffe, it was evident that Takali was in a state of chaos. The Germans had been lucky with direct hits and the bigger bombs dropped had caused a great deal of damage. Their impact had blown the protective walls of the blast-pens on to the aircraft, putting most of the new Spitfires out of action.

This was the heaviest day of bombing Malta sustained during the Second World War. It has been suggested that the crescendo of violence and destruction had been laid on, not only because of the arrival of Spitfires from the USS *Wasp*, but also in honour of Hitler's birthday.

Be that as it may, it seemed to the newcomers that it would be days before the aerodrome of Takali could be cleared. That night, however, the soldiers of the Inniskillings and the Manchesters, working flat out with arc-lamps, filled in the bomb-holes with hundreds of tons of stones. They flattened and rolled the aerodrome and cleared it of debris. By first light Takali was operational again.[8]

That day Malta's Governor General sent a telegram to the Chiefs of Staff:

The primary need is Spitfires and more Spitfires. They must not arrive in driblets, but in really big quantities. . . At all costs we cannot avoid the danger of our fighter force being worn down before the convoys arrive so that it will not be strong enough to protect it on arrival. . . If Malta is to be held drastic action is needed now. It is a question of survival.[9]

In the meantime David Douglas-Hamilton made arrangements for the pilots of his Squadron to fly with the most experienced pilots in Malta of 249 Squadron to learn "the Malta form". He himself was the first to go up the next morning. Only then did it come home to him that he was no longer an observer of a great human drama unfolding; he and his pilots had become participants in the grim life-and-death struggle which lay ahead.

Chapter Five

THE FIGHTER PILOT'S PARADISE

ON 21 April 1942 the pilots of 603 Squadron, who were sleeping in an olive grove, were roused by the crackle of cannon fire from ME109s strafing Takali. Most of the pilots were in tents because of lack of accommodation, and as they made their way to the Officers' Mess in the early morning sunlight, they witnessed the stark reality of the job ahead of them.

A smoking Hurricane came into view, flying at about eight hundred feet. The pilot was seen climbing out of his cockpit and jumping. His parachute streamed and would not open. Tony Holland wrote:

> We knew that many people had also witnessed this tragedy and knowing the inevitable outcome, none of us saw any point in demoralising ourselves by going to where he had struck the ground. There was nothing we could do apart from saying a short prayer for him.[1]

By 6 a.m. David and the three Flight Lieutenants in his Squadron had left the Mess and were on readiness, along with Squadron Leader Grant, the exceptional Commanding Officer of 249 Squadron, and three other pilots. Arriving at the Dispersal Hut they saw an unexploded 1000 lb bomb, lying a few feet in front of the building. They sent for help and the pilots watched behind sandbags while it was defused by Flight Lieutenant Dickinson and his assistants.

They then searched Takali for serviceable aircraft, and found six. Almost all the Spitfires flown there from the *Wasp* had been destroyed by direct hits or damaged with shrapnel holes. After putting their kit into the available aircraft, they sat down and waited. David described what happened:

> We were told the first raid generally came over at

about 8 a.m. We would fly in pair formation line abreast, crossing over in turn, climb up, and then dive on the bombers as they came in to bomb.

I got a few more tips from Johnny Plagis, an old hand, who told me how in March they had been attacking very large enemy raids with only four or six Spitfires. One day he had had to do this four times, and on each occasion had been shot at by Hun fighters whenever he tried to land. He said, "I don't believe the Battle of Britain had anything over Malta!"

We sat and waited in the first sunshine, wondering what the morning would bring. Everything seemed so peaceful and quiet. The huge dome of Musta Church was glinting and bright gold in the early sun, and here and there a Maltese peasant was gathering up bundles of hay on his cart. Across the sea one could just make out the faint outline of Sicily. We wondered what was going on over there, especially on the German aerodromes at Comiso and Catania.

Johnny gave a running commentary as to what the Germans would be doing at their bomber aerodromes at this time. Friedrich would be sitting in his JU88 running up his engine. "Hello Hans, die port engine she is OK— so is die starboard one. Die bombs dey are all on and OK! Fertig! Ja goot! You ready, Hans? You ready, Hermann? You ready, Ernst? Right, now we shall off-fly. I zink Takali again today!"

Suddenly the telephone bell rang. "Stand to" we were told. This meant climbing into the cockpit and getting strapped in, all ready. It looked as if Johnny's commentary was about synchronised with the facts.

We had not long to wait. "Scramble!" Up we climbed to about 30,000 feet, joining up with another party of Spitfires and Hurricanes from the other aerodromes. From that height Malta looked about the size of a large penny. It was easy to lose sight of it under one's wing-tip. Sicily, however, seemed very large and hostile with Mount Etna sitting up at the back of it. For the rest, there was nothing but miles and miles of unfriendly sea all round.

Then we saw AA burst below, and dived down towards them. Aircraft suddenly started whirling all round, and I and another of my pilots got separated from the others. Not knowing the 'Malta form' we dived down in the wrong direction and missed the bombers. So we tried an abortive chase after some 109s, but were too far behind them and could not catch up. We did not fire our guns at all that time.

But that did not happen again for many a day; every flight for some time after that we got a shot at something.

The others, however, had contacted the bombers and had destroyed one or two JU88s, a 109, and damaged some more. All the Spitfires came back undamaged. When we came in to land we saw a stick of large bomb-holes right across the aerodrome, but managed to pick an extra large gap between two craters and got down all right.

Johnny Plagis and another pilot circled the aerodrome, covering us while we landed; for there were 109s about, waiting for an opportunity to pounce on us while landing.

We loitered down on the aerodrome for some time. Bill had been in a gun-pit with Jack Satchell, who had been firing twin Vickers guns at the 88s as they came down. Jack had already hit and damaged over a dozen of them in various raids. We then climbed into the bus to go up to the Mess. The air-raid siren had already gone again.

As we left, the red flag—a take cover signal—went up, and we had not yet reached the boundary of the aerodrome when we heard the whistle and crash of bombs. They sounded near, and we lay flat on the bottom of the bus. They were ME109 fighter bombers. At the first opportunity we leapt out and crouched in a nearby bomb-hold while more bombs came down. Then we looked up and saw the 88s approaching the aerodrome.

We just had time to reach a proper air-raid shelter nearby when the heavy bombs came down. We stood at the bottom of the shelter while the blitz raged above, and bomb after bomb was heard whistling down and exploding. We talked—cracking jokes and laughing incessantly. This was the form our nervous reaction took. I smoked pipe after pipe, and wished I was in the air again. At last it was all over and we continued on our way. There was one more heavy raid that day on Takali, and a few more of the Squadron flew.[2]

The Commander of 601 County of London Squadron, Squadron Leader John Bisdee, taking off from Luqa, made contact with the enemy and saw the Junkers 88 he was firing at puff with smoke. He was then shot down five miles out at sea. He had baled out and paddled back to Malta in a dinghy. And so it was that the first day ended, with the pilots at Takali having only four serviceable aircraft remaining, and the other aerodromes only two more. On 22 April only six Spitfires remained operational out of the forty-six brought to the island, and as quickly as others were repaired, at least as many were damaged, if not by enemy gunfire, then by running into one of the countless bomb holes.[3]

In the morning Flying Officer Tony Holland, and Pilot Officers Murray from the USA and Linton from Canada, were scrambled, led by the Canadian Buck McNair of 249 Squadron. It was during this flight that the Edinburgh Squadron had its first loss. In the distance some Junkers 88s were seen diving towards an aerodrome, but McNair would not be drawn. The young American, Murray, went for them on his own, an action involving much risk and great courage. He was never seen again, probably shot down over the Mediterranean by a large number of Messerschmitt 109s.

On arrival back at Takali, the whole aerodrome was covered in bomb craters, concentrated around the centre of the landing strip. Pilot Officer Linton landed over the craters and careered through the fence, ending up on his nose. Holland, anxious to avoid this fate, landed short and plunged into a bomb crater. After this McNair was not allowed to land at Takali and was sent to Luqa. Later

Flight Sergeant Johnny Hurst was scrambled, and reported that he had probably destroyed an ME109.[4]

In the afternoon Flight Lieutenant Bill Douglas took the remaining serviceable Spitfire from Takali to Luqa, and was scrambled with 126 Squadron. One of the new pilots, Frank Jemmet, was shot up, crash-landed, and died in hospital. That morning he had been so proud that he was going to fly a Spitfire in action for the first time. The Maltese girl in the house where he had been billeted had had a premonition. When he came into the room, a bead had run away from the rosary in her hand.[5]

Wing Commander Gracie heard that a Maltese had stolen Frank Jemmett's parachute, depriving him of the opportunity of baling out, which might have saved his life. At the end of the month Gracie took over from Jack Satchell as Station Commander, and gave orders for a gibbet to be erected on the aerodrome, as a warning to anybody else who might try to steal a fighter pilot's parachute. He was never given cause to put his threat into practice, and the incident earned for him the reputation of being a hard man.[6]

Later the same day some bitter verses appeared on the Officers' Mess notice board, called "Kesselring's Easter Hymn", to commemorate the 1942 Easter weekend in Malta.

Tis Holy Thursday, let us snooker
All the bloody Spits at Luqa
Forward Messerschmitt and Stuka

                        Hallelujah.

Hail Good Friday, Hal Far's turn,
Prang the crews, the aircraft burn,
Will the blighters never learn

                        Hallelujah.

Now Kampfgeschwaders, rise and shine
Make Takali toe the line
Here a rocket, there a mine

                        Hallelujah.

Christ the Lord is risen today
Let's bomb the harbour, bomb the bay,

Bomb the bloody place all day

Hallelujah.

Easter Monday, so ply the whip
Smite the island thigh and hip
Tear if off a Safi strip[7]

Hallelujah.

That day, 22 April, a telegram from Air Marshal
Tedder, marked "Most Secret", reached the Chief of the
Air Staff. It confirmed that after the arrival of the Spitfires
from the USS *Wasp*, the Luftwaffe had attacked within
ninety minutes, and within three days had dropped more
than five hundred tons of bombs on Takali and Luqa
aerodromes, with more than four hundred landing on
Takali alone. The German intention was to bring Malta to
submission by air blockade, destroying the aerodromes,
the aircraft and equipment and the harbour facilities to
prevent any convoy landing.

The defence would only have six to eight Spitfires
available, for each sortie, since nine had been destroyed
on the ground by bombs, and another twenty-nine had
been damaged by bomb splinters in their blast-pens
sufficiently badly to make them unserviceable. Another
eight Spitfires had been destroyed in combat and seventy-
five per cent of the rest had been damaged in the aerial
fighting. Further damage to the small number remaining
was likely from landing and taking off among the bomb
holes. As for the Wellington bombers, some had been
destroyed and others damaged.

The telegram ended on the ominous note that it would
not be possible to run a convoy to Malta before the air
situation was satisfactory, as it would be destroyed in
harbour. Malta needed a hundred Spitfires a month: an
abundance of Spitfires was necessary to hold the island
and, after landing, they must be put back into the air
before the next raid arrived.[8]

Winston Churchill acted on this information by putting
President Roosevelt in the picture, albeit with another
request:

I am deeply anxious about Malta under the unceasing bombardment of 450 first-line German aircraft. If the island fortress is to hold out till the June convoy which is the earliest possible, it must have a continued flow of Spitfires. The last flying off from *Wasp* was most successful although unhappily the enemy's attack broke up many after they had landed.

We are using *Eagle* to send in 15 or so at a time. I shall be grateful if you will allow *Wasp* to do a second trip . . . Without this I fear Malta will be pounded to bits.[9]

Back at Takali the fighter pilots were making the best of their lot. The 25 April was an eventful day, with three raids of about one hundred German aircraft each. The strain on some of the pilots was beginning to tell. Johnny Johnston was scrambled for the second raid, and was following a Junkers 88 when he was attacked by some six ME109s, who dived on him again and again. As he kept turning, watching the cannon shells flicker past, he began to tire, until his Spitfire went into a spin. When he pulled out alone, he felt exhausted.

He heard a call over the radio from Group Captain Woodhall asking him to cover the landing of a damaged Spitfire at Takali. At first he was too tired to reply. He eventually responded, knowing that when the Fighter Pilot was driven to the limit of human endurance he was still expected to do more if necessity demanded.[10]

At 5.41, no less than fifty-seven Junkers 88s, twenty-seven Junkers 87s, and a large escort of ME109s attacked. Outnumbered by more than ten to one, six Hurricanes and three Spitfires took off, with Flight Lieutenant Douglas and Sergeant Webster flying the two Spitfires from Takali. They dived on the Junkers 88s, Douglas shooting down one and Webster damaging another. This was the first confirmed victory for Edinburgh Squadron but Webster's aircraft was damaged by an exploding bomb, and he had to crash-land.[11]

Just what it was like, going into such an attack, was indicated in a graphic description of his activities late that afternoon by Pilot Officer Paul Brennan, DFC, an exceptional Australian pilot in 249 Squadron.

> Five hundred yards away, and dead in front of us, was an 88 . . . More 109s were coming down on me, but they were still out of range. I decided to take a chance and try to deal with my 88 before the 109s were on me. As I closed in the 88's rear-gunner opened fire . . . I was so excited and so keen to get the 88 before the 109s forced me to break away, that I was unaware that his bullets were hitting my aircraft.
>
> I continued diving straight at him, until I was only 250 yards behind him. Then I opened fire with all four cannon. The rear-gunner stopped firing. I concentrated my fire now against the 88's two motors and the pilot's glasshouse. I could see my shells crashing into him, and in a few seconds he started to smoke. I was acutely conscious of the 109s diving on me, and knew that if I waited to check my aim, I would be cold meat for them . . . I kept on firing . . . He caught fire and started to disintegrate.[12]

That was good enough for Brennan. On coming down to land, his Spitfire was rocked by the explosion of bombs below, and he landed pulling up just before a bombhole. When he looked over his Spitfire he found ten bullet holes, one through the prop, six inches away from his head. They were all living close to death.[13]

Approximately five German aircraft had been destroyed and about nine damaged, for the loss of one Hurricane, and a few others with bullet holes or other damage. This was the approximate overall ratio during the raids. Besides there was always the possibility of repairing damaged Spitfires and Hurricanes landing on Malta, or of cannibalising them for spare parts. No such possibility existed for those German aircraft which had been damaged, and which crash-landed in the sea on the way back to Sicily. The Spitfire pilots seldom knew exactly how many they shot down. As David Douglas-Hamilton wrote:

When attacking such large numbers with so many enemy fighters about, one could not afford to stay long behind an enemy aircraft, so one used to "squirt" at as many as possible without waiting to see the results, and then get safely back on the ground again.[14]

Morale was high, and that night David wrote home to his wife, showing the high spirits of the fighter pilots in Malta.

I have now been on this island for five days, and I must say it is a somewhat different life from any I have known before. You will have gathered from the Press and News that we have raids every day and pretty heavy ones at that, but this place still holds out and it will continue to hold out . . .

For the first time I have heard the whistle and explosion of a bomb so clearly that I will never forget it! The boys here are simply marvellous—they have shot down masses of Huns for virtually no loss—it is a real honour to be with such chaps.

We too are lacing into them and one of the Squadron, Bill Douglas, got a Hun today. My respect for the German pilots has gone down considerably— they are scared stiff of Spitfires! . . . I have lived through many adventures already, but it has been great fun really and I must say I have enjoyed it all greatly . .

England seems very far away just now, and so does the life I used to lead.[15]

Back in London an important development had taken place. The Prime Minister had sent a note to the Chief of the Air Staff. It consisted of one sentence, which said everything that needed to be said: "Now that the President has agreed about *Wasp* let me know the programme for feeding Malta with Spitfires, week by week, during the next eight weeks".[16]

David had no knowledge of this when on 30th April he was again in the thick of the fighting. He and his pilots had been sent out to intercept a raid, and been ordered to gain height quickly out to sea. David's account recorded the words Group Captain Woodhall used and what followed:

"Big jobs (bombers) now fifteen miles north of Grand Harbour coming south. Many little jobs (fighters) over the island." Then later: "Party has now split into three and are coming in over St. Paul's Bay, Grand Harbour, and Kalafrana." At the right moment he said, "Come in now, and come in fast."

Down we went at about 400 mph into the middle of the 88s, just as they finished their dive. We rapidly closed with them head on and "squirted" one after another. Johnny Hurst destroyed one and John Buckstone damaged another. I "squirted" three 88s and a 109. Others had been shot at and quite possibly damaged, but we had not time to wait and see. One of my cannon had jammed and both Neville King's refused to fire. One of John Buckstone's had also jammed. We found later that some of the ammunition was faulty.

Then the 109s came down on us, and we pulled this way and that. I remember being shot at on five occasions as I turned around, each time being thankful I had seen the Hun in time and watching the tracer passing behind me.

We became split up, but re-formed over the aerodrome, and then we had the longest part of the fight waiting to land. Round and round we went, a few feet above the ground, watching the 109s circling above and waiting for the unwary.

Suddenly I saw a 109 coming straight for me. He was very low, just above the ground. As I turned I saw his tracer come out. Jack Satchell also saw it from behind his twin Vickers' guns and he let fly at it, hitting it all along the fuselage. It came down in the sea just off the coast. Eventually the 109s made off, and we all got down without a scratch, though Johnny Hurst had been shot up and we were all perspiring freely. I felt as if I had just played a strenuous Rugger match.

In landing again lay one of our chief problems; for the Hun fighters always circled around about 3000 feet above us when we wanted to land, and if anyone was foolish enough to attempt a landing while they were about, they would "pounce" on him and shoot him up.

I saw this happen to one of our pilots (Tony Holland) one day as he came in with wheels and flaps down. Fortunately a nearby Bofors gun crew also saw it, and made the 109 pull up by pumping its red tracer at him.

A little later it happened to me. I had seized what I thought was propitious moment for landing after a raid, having looked carefully all round and seen nothing. Lowering my wheels and flaps I concentrated on the landing. I throttled back a little earlier than usual as I straightened up on the glide, and to my surprise heard the rattle of musketry coming from the ground. Forthwith I started to turn, but barely had time to look behind me when I saw the large round nose of a ME109 pass just a few feet behind me. Luckily for me he was a bad shot, as I did not get a single bullet-hole in my aircraft. But his bullets had surprised several people on the ground as much as he had surprised me, and some of them had narrow escapes.

Sometimes the Huns would keep us up extra long, while we circled the aerodrome, by sending in relays of 109s from Sicily. They generally had to leave before we got too low in petrol, but on one occasion a Spitfire ran out of petrol as it finished its landing run. It was exciting to say the least of it!

One day towards the end of April we had just had a large raid by 88s and 87s with their usual diving tactics on the three aerodromes, when a new lot of bombers started coming in. There were five of them in beautiful "Vic" formation, and we all wondered when they would start their dive and what place they would bomb. But they did not dive at all, and presently we heard a sort of warbling, hissing sound that turned out to be their bombs falling—quite unlike the usual

77

whistle of German bombs.

The general consensus of opinion decided that they were "Eyeties". This was confirmed later when some of them were shot down. Their escorting fighters flew in very pretty but unwarlike close formation. To keep such formation they obviously had to concentrate rather hard to keep position, which precluded their looking about them for our fighters. In due course they learnt their lesson through bitter experience after we had shot many of them down.

Thus ended April: an epic month in the second siege of Malta. Over 6500 tons of bombs were dropped on the island in this month, more than 500 of them on one day alone. It was more than the whole of Britain had received in any one month of the blitz. The morale of some of the people had fallen to a certain extent, and one occasionally saw the word *"Pace"* (Peace) chalked up; but on the whole it was still high—a truly remarkable fact after the battering Malta had received, and the words "Bomb Rome" were frequently painted on walls.

The Germans, of course, could not know this, and were fully justified in thinking that Malta was on its last legs. Some pilots who had seen a German pilot in hospital reported the following words from him: "Today—I prisoner; in two months you, you, you, and you prisoner—I free!" [17]

During the heavy bombing the Germans had inevitably succeeded in cutting down Malta's offensive powers while convoys were sent across to Rommel. But it had cost them dearly. Throughout April the island's defences had destroyed at least 150 enemy aircraft—fifty by fighters and a hundred by AA. Counting probables, the total was well over two hundred.

No words of praise can be too high for the AA gunners. Some of them were Maltese, but most were British soldiers who had been in Malta some years and had seen all its "blitzes". They had borne the brunt of the April bombing and had been dive-bombed time and again. Sometimes their gun positions were hit, but those who remained carried on just the same. On several occasions they had saved RAF pilots trying to land. The only trouble was that at the end of April they were running out of ammunition, and were limited to a few rounds each day.

The aerial war was bitter and merciless, as is usually the case when the Germans are on top. They used to shoot up our pilots baling out or sitting in life-saving dinghies, and the air sea rescue launch. Things had changed radically since the first Christmas of the war with Italy, when the Italians had dropped Christmas cards on Takali aerodrome.

Naturally, the island's score would have been much higher had we had more fighters and been able to maintain them on the ground. There were plenty of targets for any number of Spitfires and plenty of different types to choose from—JU88s and 87s, ME109s, Macchis, Reggianes, Savoias and many others. In fact, Malta was justly named "The Fighter Pilot's paradise".[18]

On 1 May David had a personal success. With three of his pilots he was scrambled at 5p.m. to intercept Italian bombers, but they came across ME109s instead. Two ME109s attacked Sergeant Rae and John Buckstone. The control column of Rae's Spitfire was shot away, and he was hit in the leg. He parachuted and the wind blew him over the sea to Malta. He found himself threatened by a Maltese farmer with a shotgun, until the farmer realised that he was a Spitfire pilot and left no doubt in Rae's mind as to where Maltese sympathies lay.

In the space of three seconds David had fired more than a dozen cannon shells at the 109 that had shot up Sergeant Rae. Then he followed Rae down to protect him while he was in his parachute. John Buckstone put a cannon shell through the 109's tail and Ken Mitchell squirted twice. Later the 109 was seen going into the sea. That night none of the three men put in a claim, perhaps because each thought the other would do it. But the fact remained plain and unmistakable. An ME109 at which they had fired had disappeared into the sea.

On 3 May Bill Douglas shot the cockpit off a Stuka, and Pilot Officer Slade found that his cannons would not fire, but still managed to shoot down a JU87 with his machine guns. His experience and that of other pilots led to a close examination of the Spitfire cannons and ammunition. On the 4 May they learnt that virtually one-third of all cannon rounds were misfits, which would cause jamming. This caused considerable annoyance and reports were sent back to the Air Ministry.

That day Norman MacQueen, a Flight Commander of 249 Squadron who had shot down about eight Axis aircraft, and who was much liked by the other pilots, was killed. David wrote:

> Several of us saw it happen from the Mess verandah. Norman was flying with another Spitfire and about to attack some 109s, when we saw a 109 sweeping across the sky behind him. Vainly we shouted, "Turn! Spit!" as if there was some hope that he might hear us. But evidently neither of them saw the 109 and just kept straight on. We saw the 109's tracer going right into Norman's machine. His Spitfire lurched and gave out a thin smoke trail. For some time it seemed to be under control and circled downwards as if he hoped to land. Then suddenly the nose went forward, and the machine dived like a stone into the ground, bursting into flames as it hit. I felt a lump come into my throat. [19]

MacQueen's radio had not been working, and he did not hear the warning before he was shot down. His loss came home to the other pilots when his bed and personal kit, including the photograph of his girl friend, were removed. [20] Tony Holland described the effects of air warfare on the morale of the pilots:

> We were certainly well keyed up and rearing to have

a go, but one cannot deny having rapidly built up a shell to insulate one's feelings as lively and cheerful friends disappeared with the utter finality of death, and a somewhat numbed perseverance took over. Laughter came a little less readily as time went on. There was no question of bolstering up our spirits in wild mess parties. There were no bar stocks.[21]

Some of the more experienced fighter pilots were suffering from intense strain. Johnny Johnston was sleeping irregularly and was lying awake at night, and although he thought that others were in a similar position, he could not talk about it to anyone. The tension was always present. He wrote:

> When the difference between a cannon shell over your head and a cannon shell in the cockpit represented an immeasurably short space on a German reflector-sight, or an immeasurably short time in a German head, it was beginning to be terrifying to believe that your fate depended on your own vigilance, and yet terrible to think of it in the blind capricious hands of chance . . . [22]

The Maltese too knew that the island's fate hung in the balance, and depended on the outcome of the battle being waged in the air. Paul Brennan noticed this and wrote:

> Whenever we ventured into Valletta or visited one of the island's other towns . . . haggard faces would break into a smile, and a cheery word would greet us. They never failed to show the admiration they felt for the fighter pilots defending the island.[23]

By this time the defence forces were well aware that at the end of April some three strips had been cleared near Gerbini airfield in the Vale of Catania, Sicily, for gliders. Each strip was close to a railway system, and it was clear that preparations were in hand for a massive airborne invasion of Malta.

What was even more disturbing was that German gliders could be transferred in sections by rail, and could quickly be assembled, and that large camps existed nearby to accommodate thousands of troops.[24]

Although they were fighting back, the pilots in Malta were being worn down by a process of attrition. The day and night bombing prevented them and the British and Maltese anti-aircraft gunners from getting the necessary ration of sleep. There was never enough food, and tempers became frayed.[25]

That was the atmosphere on 4 May, when Wing Commander Gracie, as Station Commander, addressed the pilots at Takali. He told them that the new Spitfires were on the way, and would arrive on 9 May. He wanted every one of them to be back in the air within fifteen minutes. This talk made all the pilots more determined.[26]

On the same day Winston Churchill was preoccupied with Malta, and signed three memoranda. One instructed Lord Gort to go to Malta straight away. Another stated that if the George Cross was not ready it should be sent on as fast as possible for Lord Gort to present to the Maltese people. The third was a generous message to General Dobbie relieving him, and thanking him for his selfless and highminded spirit, and devotion to the public interest.[27]

Churchill knew how much was at stake, since he had read a Report that if air superiority over Malta could be attained, it would be possible to "whistle up" bombers from the Middle East and operate them from Malta against Sicilian aerodromes. He hoped desperately that the second USS *Wasp* Malta Relief Force with HMS *Eagle* would be able to turn the balance.

Two days later, on 6 May, Johnny Johnston went down. He was firing at an ME109, but did not hear another behind him until three cannon shells exploded in his Spitfire. As the machine plunged in a spin towards the ground, with flames roaring up from the bottom of the cockpit, he corrected the spin, unlocked the locking pin of his harness, threw his stick forward, and was shot forward into the air. Somehow his parachute opened, and as he lay smouldering on the ground, half conscious, his face in blood and sand, a crowd of sympathetic Maltese gathered. He heard somebody asking if he was dead and was taken to Mtarfa hospital, where his arms and face were covered in bandages.[28]

On 7 May when General Lord Gort VC arrived in Malta, there were only six Spitfires capable of operational flights. He intervened immediately, as he also knew that the considerable interval between the arrival of Spitfires and their preparation for battle was far too long, and had enabled the Luftwaffe to bomb Spitfires on the ground before they could be turned round and be put back in the air.

Lord Gort overcame the doubts of Air Vice Marshal Lloyd and the Admiral by insisting on two matters. The Spitfires landing must be refuelled and rearmed within twenty minutes, with Army assistance. Also any ship coming into harbour must be protected by a smoke-screen.[29]

Wing Commander Gracie also believed that the system should be streamlined so that a reinforcement of Spitfires would be speedily reserviced. Plans were made accordingly, in the hope that Malta would hold out until the next Spitfire reinforcement.

Preparations at the aerodromes were completed for such an arrival. Every blast-pen had to have enough fuel and ammunition. Those who had to fill the bomb holes in the runway, the Bren gun carriers who had to pull damaged aircraft to one side, and the stretcher bearers, all received their orders, the Army and the Royal Air Force working hand in hand.[30]

David's account continued:

We did not do much flying owing to the shortage of aircraft, and time was spent making ready for the new arrivals. We were not going to be caught out on the ground this time, and prepared for a quick turn-round when the new aircraft landed. All hands were belting ammunition and placing dumps of fuel into slit trenches beside each aircraft pen.

We were down on the aerodrome one day (8 May) doing this when an alert was sounded. No fighters were up; and Takali had not been raided for nearly a week, so we had a nasty suspicion it might be our turn now. About six of us took rifles and repaired to a disused gun-pit on the aerodrome. Presently the "flak" went up and we saw a party of JU87s coming towards us from the north. "Looks like us this time", someone said. But the 87s seemed to go past as if making for somewhere else. They got well behind and up-sun of us, and then turned and started to dive.

We had no time to think, but fired our rifles at the first one as they dived down one after another. Then came the bombs. The sound they made was more like a warbling, tearing shriek than a whistle. They were very close. Out of the corner of my eye I could see them flit past just before they hit the ground a few yards away. Then an earthquake occurred and a large mass of earth fanned up.

Several stones fell into our pit. "Thank God for my tin hat!" I thought as some stones fell on it. I was glad I had a rifle; it gave me something to do. I worked feverishly at reloading and aimed at the belly of an 87, allowing for what I thought was ample deflection. Bomb after bomb was coming down; there seemed no end to them. At this point I was no longer looking up and firing at the 87s coming down. I was kneeling, sitting on my heels, firing at them as they went by.

Then as suddenly as it had begun, the attack ceased. We stood up and watched the 87s going back to Sicily, apparently none the worse for our efforts. No one was hurt, although several had had large stones on tin hats, but all our hearts were beating at several times the normal rate. Probably the actual attack did not last much more than five minutes, but it seemed interminable.[31]

The Spitfire pilots might perhaps have been forgiven for wondering whether reinforcements would really arrive in time. In David's case, he knew that the British had always fought against any foreign power seeking to obtain dominance over Central Europe. His great grandfather, Lieutenant Augustus Hamilton, had served in the Mediterranean on board the British flagship the *Victory*, alongside Admiral Lord Nelson, one hundred and thirty eight years before. With good cause Nelson had then written "Malta is in my thoughts, sleeping and waking".[32]

Those had been the days when the British fleet had stood in the way of Napoleon's dictatorship, which threatened to spread beyond European shores. Indeed shortly before Trafalgar Nelson had sent his famous signal, "Now I can do no more. We must put our trust in the great Disposer of Events, and in the justice of our cause." The whole of the British fleet had cheered.[33]

But on 8 May 1942 there was no fleet in Malta. The overwhelming power of the Luftwaffe had driven the British Navy hundreds of miles away, leaving the RAF outnumbered by more than ten to one. All that stood between the starving population in Malta and the planned invasion supported by six hundred or more Axis aircraft in Sicily, were a few lightly armed soldiers, the Maltese and British anti-aircraft gunners, the fighter pilots, about a dozen Hurricanes, and six Spitfires.

Still the British fleet was not completely defeated. Late that day one solitary ship was making its way past Algiers in the direction of Malta. It was the fast minelayer HMS *Welshman*, loaded up with her vital cargo of anti-aircraft ammunition and spare parts for Spitfires. She had been sent by the Admiralty, with Churchill's approval, in the certain knowledge that she might never make it.[34]

But the British Navy had a powerful friend. At the western end of the Mediterranean were a number of British destroyers, with the small British aircraft carrier HMS *Eagle*, and in front of it the giant American carrier *Wasp*, the two between them carrying sixty-four Spitfires. Winston Churchill, dreading the possibility of Malta being "pounded to bits", had asked Roosevelt to permit the *Wasp* to deliver "another good sting", and the President had responded.[35] This force was moving slowly eastwards towards the small island which by all logic, common sense and reason could not expect to survive.

That night David received his orders. It was to be his Squadron which was to fly the remaining Spitfires to cover the approach of the incoming fighter force. This responsibility he gave to John Buckstone, who only a few weeks before had said that it looked as if Malta had had it. By nightfall every pilot knew what he had to do.

Chapter Six
THE VICTORY OF 10th MAY

AFTER the almost complete destruction of the first USS *Wasp* Malta Relief Force by the massive German bombing raids, the starving lightly-armed defence forces of the island fortress would have found it virtually impossible to withstand an Invasion force in late April or in early May 1942. Even Field Marshal Kesselring admitted that it would have been easy to capture the island after the bombing assault.

Field Marshal Rommel went even further. He believed that the German High Command had made a fundamental strategic error in invading Greece and then Crete, rather than Malta. He would have much preferred it if the Luftwaffe contingents in Greece and Crete had been concentrated on Malta, so as to protect convoy traffic to the Afrika Korps in North Africa.

If German armed forces had disregarded Greece and Crete, and Malta had been taken, the Afrika Korps could in Rommel's view have secured the Mediterranean area and the Middle East oil reserves. Without supplies from the British Empire, Yugoslavia, Greece and Crete would have had to surrender, and Germany would have been well placed with the Middle Eastern oilfields in its possession for an attack on the Soviet Union.

Once this opportunity had been missed, in 1941, Kesselring and Rommel knew that the War was becoming one of logistics and supply. Partly because of the bombing of Malta more supply-bearing convoys were reaching Rommel's forces, but if the RAF in Malta was allowed to recover its striking power, the position of the Afrika Korps would be precarious in the extreme.[1]

Kesselring and Rommel knew that if Germany was to win the War in the Mediterranean and North Africa, Malta would sooner or later have to be destroyed as a British Commonwealth base. But on 1 May, when Hitler and Mussolini met at Berchtesgaden to discuss the Malta

Invasion Plans, Hitler said that the attack in the desert should have precedence over the invasion of Malta, and that the latter could take place in mid-July.[2]

So certain was the German Armed Forces High Command that Malta had been neutralised by the bombing, that arrangements were made to transfer forty-five fighters and forty dive-bombers to North Africa. A further bomber group and a fighter group were sent to Russia.[3]

At the streak of first light on 9 May, almost before these arrangements were completed, Spitfires were taking off from the USS *Wasp* and from HMS *Eagle.* Not all of the new Spitfires made the journey successfully. Of forty-seven flying off the USS *Wasp,* the first lost power while taking off and plunged into the sea, another came down in the sea, a third crashed on the African coast, and Pilot Officer Smith flying a fourth had an unusual adventure.

By mistake Smith had jettisoned his auxiliary tank, and contrary to the strictest orders flew back to land on the *Wasp.* By a remarkable piece of airmanship he landed his Spitfire on board without naval arresting gear. He wanted to take a new tank and set off for Malta, but as the task force was moving back to Gibraltar, permission was denied. The American Captain was so pleased that his landing had been successful that for once there was a round of strong drink, breaking American naval tradition. Pilot Officer Smith followed his colleagues out to Malta in a Liberator a day or so later.[4]

Meanwhile the six remaining Spitfires on the island were scrambled to cover the arrival, with Flying Officer Holland flying as Number Two to John Buckstone. They climbed down sun from East to West on the south side of the island, and they were attacked by numerous ME109s at about 16,000 feet. Holland wrote:

> As they passed us, we all fired at them, and John was either hit in their attack, or I think more likely followed one down too far and too fast. I saw the 109 go into the water with a great dirty green splash and John Buckstone's Spitfire hit the water seconds later with a

big clean white splash—I remember thinking the colours were almost symbolic at the time, and the position of the white splash relative to his dive could have indicated he was trying to pull out but did not make it.[5]

During the encounter Holland and Pilot Officer Ken Mitchell shot down an ME109, and escorted the first of the fifty-nine incoming Spitfires, which arrived at 10 a.m. David was watching on the ground and recorded that:

Soon the air was filled with a great mass of Spitfires coming in. What a wonderful sight! To say we welcomed them put one's feelings mildly. They landed one by one, and our covering section also landed, having done their job. So John Buckstone had gone! It was hard to believe we should not see him again and be cheered by his lively humour.[6]

Twenty-three Spitfires had arrived at Takali aerodrome, the other thirty-six going to Luqa and Hal Far. This time the new Spitfires were refuelled, rearmed and put back into the air within ten minutes. The last came in before 11 a.m. and they too were back in the air within a few minutes.

603 (City of Edinburgh Squadron) now had twelve Spitfires and was split up into three sections, the Red section being led by David Douglas-Hamilton, White section being led by Bill Douglas, and Blue section by Flight Lieutenant Sanders.

Blue section was scrambled at 12 o'clock. Tony Holland remembered his second flight that day, which taught his Squadron how important it was to have well-serviced aircraft.

As soon as he was airborne he found that his radio would not work. This gave him a feeling of being deaf and mute, and he anxiously scanned horizons for targets and attackers. While he was doing this he lost his Section at 24,000 feet.

Assuming that Blue Section had dived, he determined

to catch up, and pushed the nose down in a rapid dive with full throttle, the air speed indicator needle reaching far beyond its marked readings. Shock waves built up, causing the control column to buffet, so that he could not hold it steady. Gradually he managed to ease his Spitfire out of his near vertical dive, and to his delight saw three aircraft ahead of him, which he imagined to be Blue section. He closed rapidly, and suddenly realised that they were Messerschmitt 109s. He checked the instruments, made sure the safety catch was off the firing button, and swept in behind the nearest 109.

As soon as he was close and in a position in which he could not miss, with the 109's shape filling his gunsights, he opened fire with all four cannon, expecting to see it explode, but his guns all jammed. The next moment he shot past underneath his prey, who saw him. With a dead radio and jammed cannons Holland did not wait for them to follow. Putting his Spitfire into a controlled spiral, he landed at Takali.[7]

Shortly after his landing, while the aircraft were being refuelled, and the other pilots were having "a stand-to sweltering in the cockpits under the hot sun", six or ten Junkers 88s suddenly swooped down on the aerodrome. David Douglas-Hamilton jumped out of his Spitfire and thrust his face to the ground, and the other pilots sprinted to slit trenches. Within seconds deafening explosions surrounded them, and the pilots gasped in dust-laden air. A 500 kilogram bomb had exploded twenty feet away from a slit trench full of pilots and ground crew, but had done no harm apart from leaving "a few shattered nerves".

Two Spitfires were perforated with shrapnel, and the Edinburgh Squadron's pilots were relieved to be scrambled early in the afternoon. It was preferable to be in the air, with opportunities to shoot down Axis bombers, than to be bombed out of existence on the ground. They missed the bombers, who went to Luqa this time, and Tony Holland shot up an ME109 circling Takali.

After landing and refuelling, David's section was

scrambled in error, and climbed to 12,000 feet, but could see "nothing but Spitfires". They landed and then the German bombers arrived. The other two sections had taken off to deal with them, but had missed the bombers, though Pilot Officer Slade damaged a 109 and Bill Douglas shot one down.

On landing Johnny Hurst's Spitfire was found to be shot up, Bill Douglas' aircraft ran into a bombhole, and two other Spitfires had airscrew leaks, making them unserviceable. This left the Edinburgh Squadron with eight Spitfires available for the next day.

According to David's account the anti-aircraft gunners and five Spitfire squadrons had definitely or probably destroyed fourteen Axis aircraft, damaging another fourteen. It was quite enough to fill the fighter pilots with confidence.[8]

One of the new arrivals posted to David's Squadron was an Englishman, Flying Officer Mitchell, who summed up his first day on Malta in these words:

The tempo of life here is just indescribable. The morale of all is magnificent— pilots, ground crews, and Army, but it is certainly tough. The bombing is continuous, on and off all day. One lives here only to destroy the Hun and hold him at bay; everything else, living conditions, sleep, food, and all the ordinary standards of life have gone by the board. It all makes the Battle of Britain and fighter sweeps seem like child's play in comparison, but it is certainly history in the making, and nowhere is there aerial warfare to compare with this.[9]

That night in Sicily, Field Marshal Kesselring realised the full importance of the fact that Malta had been reinforced with a small but powerful batch of Spitfires. He reacted like a giant whose big toe had been bitten to the bone. Malta would be bombed all night and a large bombardment would be planned for the next day, although he did not have as many aircraft available as he had had at the end of April.

But even as these plans were being hatched, the Royal Navy's solitary HMS *Welshman* was still making its way to Malta, despite many narrow escapes, and laden with anti-aircraft ammunition. Meanwhile continuous bombing by Junkers 87s and 88s throughout the night allowed the Spitfire pilots little sleep.

At 5.35am. the *Welshman* crept into harbour. Unloading her supplies of ammunition started at once, with Spitfires patrolling constantly. Indeed the Spitfire pilots had been on readiness from 5a.m. Threading their way to their aeroplanes in between the periodic explosions of the delayed actions, they were delighted to see how small the damage from the night bombing had been.

At about 11a.m. came news of a big raid on its way to Malta, and along with other squadrons, David's squadron scrambled. He wrote:

The Germans were evidently going to make for the *Welshman* in the harbour, which was now covered by a thick smoke-screen and was invisible. There were about ten 88s and twenty 87s with a large escort of 109s, but for once we were meeting them on almost equal terms.

Then the harbour barrage went up. It was a stupendous sight, and put to shame all other efforts at 'flak' which anyone had seen over Malta or France. An almost solid cone of AA burst rose over the harbour from ground level to about 7000 feet. Into this the Huns were diving. Into it, too, the Spitfires dived, chasing the Huns. It never occurred to any of us that we might just as easily get hurt. In fact, it was with some irritation that I watched an 87 I was making for in front of me blown to pieces by a direct hit. Afterwards it turned out that two of the squadron's pilots, Tony Holland and Johnny Hurst, received slight gashes in their machines from shrapnel, and a pilot in another squadron had had to bale out.

We passed out of the barrage, chasing the 87s. I picked out my victim. It was a 109 crossing my front, He was in my sights now. Right!—quarter deflection and press the button. Brr! About five shots came out from each gun, but no more. The 109 saw me and did the one thing a fighter pilot should never do—he turned away, leaving me a dead astern shot. I pressed the button again, but nothing happened, Cursing my luck, I went back and had another try, this time at an 87, but all four cannon had jammed.

The air was full of Spitfires—a marvellous sight after what we had been used to, and as far as one could see out to sea there were 87s, each with a Spitfire on its tail. So I felt pretty safe going home alone, and in any case I was very angry.

I flew straight and level, and had almost reached the aerodrome, when suddenly I heard the unmistakable sound of very close cannon-fire above the noise of the engine. I turned sharply to see what it was, and a 109 passed overhead. He had been firing at me, a "sitting target" going straight and level; but I was in luck again. He must have been a very bad shot, for I had not a scratch on my aeroplane. After a while the others landed too. They had done well. Bill Douglas had probably destroyed two 87s, and Johnny Hurst one, while several more had been damaged, *four of them by Tony Holland.* [10]

Meanwhile forty tons of bombs had been dropped, one bomb just missing the *Welshman.* The German bombers and fighters had been met by thirty-seven Spitfires and thirteen Hurricanes. In the early afternoon there was another raid, but David's Squadron was held in reserve. At 5 p.m. he saw five Italian Eyeties coming in to bomb, and Spitfires shot down three of them.

Just afterwards David was scrambled for the fourth raid of the day, but had to return at once with radio transmission failure. It was fixed and he set off with the new arrival, Flying Officer Mitchell, flying as his Number Two. As the harbour barrage went up, with twenty Junkers 87s attacking the Harbour David dived down. He picked an 87, but another Spitfire was shooting at it, so he made for a 109 and gave it a long-range burst. He noticed many parachutes coming down, and thought that the

German pilots were baling out, until one of the German aircraft blew up with "a terrific explosion". These were parachute mines sent up by the ground defences.

Flying Officer Mitchell recorded his own experiences on this his second day in Malta:

> The CO (David Douglas-Hamilton) dived down into the "barrage" and I followed close on him. We flew three times to and fro in the barrage, trusting to luck to avoid the flak. Then I spotted a JU87 climbing out at the fringe of the barrage and I turned and chased him. I gave him a one second burst of cannon and he broke off sharply to the left.
>
> At that moment another JU87 came up in front of my nose and I turned into him and I let him have it. His engine started to pour out black smoke and he started weaving. I kept the tit pushed hard, and after a further two to three second burst with the one cannon I had left, the other having jammed, he heeled over at 1500 feet and went into the drink.
>
> I then spotted a 109 firing at me from behind and pulled the kite round to port, and after one and a half turns got on his tail. Before I could fire, another 109 cut across my bows from the port side, and I turned straight on his tail and fired till my cannon stopped through lack of ammo. He was hit and his engine poured out black smoke, but I had to beat it as I was now defenceless and two more 109s were attacking me. I spiralled straight down to the sea at full throttle, and then weaved violently towards land with the two 109s still firing at me . . . I kept right down at nought feet and steep-turned towards them, noticing the smoke from their gun ports as I did so. After about five minutes of this I managed to throw them off. [11]

With Pilot Officer Paul Forster and Bill Douglas shooting down a JU87 between them, the Edinburgh Squadron had destroyed , or probably destroyed, six Axis aircraft and damaged another six. David estimated that owing to the joint efforts of the Spitfire pilots forty Axis aircraft had been destroyed, or probably destroyed, and a further twenty had been damaged. [12]

The Australian Paul Brennan was more specific and noted down twenty-three Axis aircraft destroyed, twenty probably destroyed, and twenty damaged, filled with holes from cannon shells. [13] That night Rome Radio broadcast that thirty-seven Axis aircraft and failed to return. [14] It asserted that forty-seven Spitfires had been eliminated, and that a strong British naval force in the Grand Harbour had been attacked. In fact, as the Luftwaffe records admit, only three Spitfires had been shot down. Only one RAF pilot was lost and HMS *Welshman* left Malta under cover of darkness that night. The Royal Air Force had recovered air superiority over the island.

Thousands of Maltese had watched, refusing to enter the air raid shelters, while the bombs fell all around. They cheered whenever a German aircraft was shot down. Brennan wrote: "When evening came the Maltese knew we had won a great victory. The gloom and depression which had hung over Malta for so long lifted and vanished." [15]

On 11 May the Headline and columns of *The Times of Malta* read:

BATTLE OF MALTA: AXIS HEAVY LOSSES
"SPITFIRES" SLAUGHTER "STUKAS"
BRILLIANT TEAM WORK OF AA GUNNERS AND RAF
63 Enemy Aircraft Destroyed or Damaged over Malta yesterday.

The last two days have seen a metamorphosis in the Battle of Malta. After two days of the fiercest aerial combat that has ever taken place over the Island the Luftwaffe, with its Italian lackeys has taken the most formidable beating that has been known since the Battle of Britain two and a half years ago . . .

Teamwork has been the watchword during all these weary months of taking a pounding, with very little else to do than grin and bear it. . . For months on end the gunners have hurled steel and defiance at the enemy . . . They have been subjected to probably the most diabolical bombing that gunners have ever known, they have been ceaselessly machinegunned; they have suffered casualties, but others have taken their places . . . Never once have they faltered . . . The people of Malta owe them a debt which is incalculable.

Since the beginning of April this Island . . . has been pounded without ceasing . . . But yesterday the boot was on the other foot. The Hun . . . set out to liquidate our aircraft on their aerodromes . . . But he got a shattering shock. Instead of being on the ground our fighters were in the air, waiting for his blood . . . At the end of the day he retired to lick gaping wounds which he had never anticipated. . . .

During the afternoon's raids, the sky looked like the outside of some fantastic wasps nest, with aircraft milling about in a breathless, hectic rough house. The noise of cannon and machine gun was all the sweeter for the fact that half at least of them were for once on our side. That being so, nobody on the ground had the slightest qualms about the result. [16]

On 11 May, Winston Churchill (forgetting that it is a bee which cannot sting twice) sent a delighted message to the Captain and ship's company of the USS *Wasp:* "Many thanks to you for all timely help. Who said a Wasp couldn't sting twice?" [17]

David Douglas-Hamilton wrote home to his wife with confidence:

We are certainly in the thick of things here and every day has its excitements, but we have the feeling that it is a great job of work and will help greatly towards winning the war. The Germans have lost all chance of capturing Malta, I believe, and I am more convinced than ever that it will hold out.

They may try and give it hell by bombing, but we are well used to that by now, and it will avail them nothing.

Further, every day we hit back at them and give them not inconsiderable losses to think about.

We console ourselves by saying that every bomb here is one less at home or against Russia; and I gather they say at home that every bomb there is one less upon Malta! [18]

He ended by saying that they were living in stirring times, on an exciting island and that he was glad to be in the forefront of the battle. Now that he was there he was involved in a struggle even more concentrated than the Battle of Britain had been.

First, Malta was a small island and an enormous tonnage of bombs had been dropped on targets within an area of seventeen miles by nine, smaller than Greater London. Secondly, in the Battle of Britain, replacement aircraft were quickly available and were delivered. This was not the case in Malta, where for much of the time there was a shortage of spare parts for damaged Spitfires. Thirdly, and most important in the Battle of Britain, fighter pilots fought on a full stomach. In Malta they were being slowly starved.

But in both battles the RAF was outnumbered by at least ten to one, except when the Germans were outmanoeuvred. In this connection Field Marshal Kesselring paid a special tribute to RAF pilots in Malta when he wrote:

The British fighters deserve recognition for their bravery and manoeuvring skill, especially in the perfect handling of their aircraft when diving from a high altitude (30,000—40,000 feet) through the middle of closed German bomber formations. [19]

Yet, unlike the Battle of Britain, the Battle of Malta was going to last very much longer. The fighter pilots might have regained air superiority, but if the Royal Navy could not re-supply the island with food, then all would have been in vain.

When David Douglas-Hamilton and Bill Douglas sat

down to eat what little supper there was in the Mess late on 10 May, they found themselves sitting next to pilots from the Canadian prairies, from the cities and farms of the USA, from Australia's outback, from the New Zealand Bush, from the South African and Rhodesian veldt, and from various parts of German-occupied Europe.[20]

As a group they were not wholly dissimilar to the old Knights of Malta, who so many centuries before had come from all over Europe to fight their crusade. But somehow the Royal Air Force had the edge over the Knights,[21] who had come from Europe's richest and most powerful families. The pilots of the RAF came from every walk of life—from factories, farms, offices and shops, and from all over the world, to fight for the cause.

During supper there were no scenes of jubilation, festivity or of self-congratulation. Instead they experienced that quietness which descends on fighting men, when they wonder if they can hold on to the decisive victory which they have obtained.[22]

Chapter Seven
FEROCIOUS ENCOUNTERS

IN spite of the overwhelming superiority in numbers of the Luftwaffe and the Italian Air Force over the Spitfire pilots in Malta, their defeat on 10 May 1942 had knocked them off balance. Count Ciano, the Italian Foreign Minister, noted in his Diary that they had "lost many feathers",[1] that Malta's anti-aircraft defence was intact, and that the interior of the island was "one solid nest of machine guns".[2] Already some of the Italians were beginning to have the most serious doubts.

On 11 May a few Spitfires of 249 Squadron flew to Sicily. Johnny Plagis became separated and was surrounded by some ten Italian fighters at sea level. Thinking "his last minute had come, he decided to sell his life dearly, so flew straight at the nearest machine with the intention of ramming it. He did not fire a shot, but the Macchi pilot, suddenly realising his number might be up too, took violent evasive action, stalled and crashed into the sea."[3]

Bill Douglas also had an adventure. He was an outstanding fighter pilot, with many successes, but this particular episode would be imprinted indelibly on the memory of every Spitfire pilot in Malta. Douglas was following an ME109, firing as he went, as was an Englishman from 603 Squadron, Pilot Officer Bairnsfather, who was equally anxious that the Messerschmitt should not be allowed to return.

There then occurred what everybody dreaded might one day happen. The two Spitfires collided in mid-air and broke up, though the pilots baled out successfully. In the distance the 109 was seen to crash. This was the only time that Spitfires collided with each other over Malta. Douglas and Bairnsfather had bruises and were taken to hospital suffering from shock. Their Squadron Leader might have been expected to be critical about the loss of two Spitfires, but the most David wrote about their attack on the 109 was —"lads were too keen to finish him off."[4]

On the next day, the 12 May, a third pilot in the Squadron was killed, the New Zealander Ken Mitchell. David had stood him down two days before after hearing he had trouble with his eyes. On 12 May Mitchell was firing at an ME109, but was surrounded by twelve of them. He kept diving, and when he was within thirty or forty feet of the water he called up on his radio, saying, "Goodbye Woody, I've had it."

The ME109 was then followed by Ray Hesselyn, also from New Zealand, who fired and missed, fired again, and fired again and again. The ME109 turned over on its back and disappeared into the sea. Hesselyn circled to see if the pilot would emerge. He did not. When Spitfires were under threat they always came to each other's assistance, albeit sometimes too late.[5]

Three of the pilots in David's Squadron were more fortunate. Flight Lieutenant Sanders, Flying Officer Mitchell and Pilot Officer Sherwood shot down two Italian aircraft. David also received other news which infuriated him: a Spitfire pilot had been shot up in his dinghy and killed.[6]

Elsewhere the Maltese were enthusiastically clearing the debris off the streets. Paul Brennan went to the shops to buy the ribbon for the Distinguished Flying Medals which he and Ray Hesselyn had received. The shopkeepers had none, but each time they were very interested to know if he was a Spitfire pilot. When he said he was, they tried to shower him with presents, which he refused with difficulty. He could not help being impressed at the atmosphere of relief and happiness in Valletta, in comparison to the grim tension of a few days before.[7]

On 14 May David experienced the disappointment of being unable to fly, and by coincidence the same day brought with it for a time a relaxation of the German bombing offensive and confirmation of the RAF's hard-won air superiority. David wrote:

It began when a single 88 with a small escort dropped a large bomb on the town of Sliema. It escaped. Then came a raid of three 88s which was intercepted about thirty miles out to sea, and two were shot down and the third damaged. After that came a fighter sweep. We were told to stand-to our aircraft, and were just walking out to them when we heard the unmistakable whistle of falling bombs. In no time we were flat on the ground, wondering as usual when and where that awful whistle would end.

The bombs, dropped by 109 fighter-bombers, landed about thirty yards from some of us, but nobody was hit. At that moment the signal to scramble was given, and I ran to my aircraft, but was met by an airman who said, "I'm afraid they've spitchered your aeroplane, sir" ("spitchered" is Maltese for "finished"). A piece of shrapnel had pierced the petrol tank, and petrol was pouring out. That was the only damage the attack did.

The next raid came in about mid-day. I had just come off "readiness" and was on the aerodrome sheltering in a slit trench. The bombers were a long time coming in, but finally three 88s were observed approaching Takali.

They had not far to go, when I saw the rear one break away with smoke streaming out of it. Then I saw Spitfires attacking, and another 88 broke away with smoke streaming from it. The leader was now just starting his dive on my end of the aerodrome, when I saw a Spitfire above it with its cannons puffing away. Almost immediately the wing of the 88 became a mass of flame; the petrol tank had been hit.

The 88 jettisoned its bombs at the edge of the aerodrome, then did a drunken swoop across the aerodrome, and one of its engines fell out. It crashed just beside the landing-ground and burned furiously with columns of black smoke. We got out of our slit trench and cheered.

I went round to look at the wreckage. It was well smashed up. The pilot was reclining backwards in the front of the wreckage, quite dead, but still grasping the control column. He had evidently been trying to control the aeroplane until the end. Soon there was little left of him or the 88. I felt quite unmoved: he had been trying to bomb me. Everyone else around the scene felt much the same, especially the Maltese. To my delight, I learnt that all these 88s were shot down by the Squadron, Johnny Hurst having got the last one.

At tea-time another raid by three 88s came over and tried to bomb Luqa. One of them got a direct hit from "flak" and spun down burning into the sea, while two of its crew baled out. Another one was sent smoking out to sea by a Spitfire, and was later confirmed as destroyed; but the third one was very determined. He came right in, dropped his bombs, and got away again. Thus seven 88s had been destroyed out of ten that approached the island. Four 109s were also destroyed and several more damaged.[8]

After 14 May no more Junker 88s appeared over Malta for several weeks, and David never saw another Stuka before he left. There were fighter sweeps, with ME109s dropping bombs, and night raids, and although these constituted a nuisance, the bombing no longer had the devastating punch it had had in April. Yet the 109s remained much in evidence, and David was involved in an unforgettable encounter on 15 May, at about 4.10p.m.:

I drew "blood" for the second time on one of these fighter sweeps. We were "stooging" around at 25,000 feet for a considerable time; it was very cold and I even got frost-bite in a finger. We were bounced once by a pair of 109s but avoided them successfully. Eventually we were told to go down. Suddenly I saw a 109 sweeping down on my No. 2. It still came on, by this time at me, and we were approaching each other head-on at great speed. I resolved not to give way before he did, and he evidently made the same resolution. We were going straight at each other, and as soon as I got my sights on him I opened fire, and kept firing. He opened fire a second afterwards.

It all happened in a flash, but when he seemed about fifty yards away I gave a violent "yank" on the stick and broke away to the right. As I did so, his port wing broke off in the middle, and he shot past under me. I turned and looked back; his aeroplane did about five flick rolls to the left and broke up. Then a parachute opened.[9]

Nearby Flight Sergeant Irwin was firing at the other 109. He hit it and it disappeared "smoking out to sea".[10]

There was then one of the many remarkable happenings which are part of the Malta story. The German pilot whom David had shot down was wounded and was taken to Mtarfa Hospital near Takali. He was put in a bed beside Johnny Johnston, who was slowly recovering from his burns. This could not have happened elsewhere. If he had been shot down on the Russian Front, he would have been lucky to survive, and certainly would not have been put in a bed in a Russian hospital, beside a Russian pilot. Similarly, no Russian pilot shot down over German-occupied Europe would have been nursed in a bed beside a Luftwaffe pilot.

But Malta was a small island with few facilities, and in Mtarfa Hospital fighter pilots who had been shooting at each other talked about their experiences while their wounds were healing. The German told Johnston that he had been flying Stukas and transferred to fighters. He had completed more than a hundred flights over Malta, shooting down three Spitfires, a Hurricane and a Blenheim bomber.

He asked Johnston whether Italian fighters were more or less formidable than ME109s, and Johnston replied that he could not recall engaging with Italians. The German roared with laughter, since Rome Radio was always claiming that the Italian Air Force had shot down many Spitfires, and now he met a Spitfire pilot who had not even seen them.

Johnny Johnston did not like having the German in the next-door bed. He could not help remembering his Czech friends Uher and Brejcha who had fought against Nazism and were dead, and he resented the fact that this was a Sudeten German, who had no feeling for Czechoslovakia and identified himself entirely with the German race.[11]

The next day, the 16 May, David, full of confidence, fired a long burst at a 109, seeing strikes, but to his disappointment it flew away. As he landed he narrowly escaped being shot up by a 109. The bombing had killed several people on the ground, and he learned that 249

Squadron had reached its century of Axis aircraft shot down over Malta. [12]

He made his way up to Mtarfa Hospital, as he wished to see his "prisoner", whom he had shot out of the sky a few hours before. David found the German pilot in bed, with his left arm in plaster, as it had been broken by a cannon shell.

> He was a small, muscular, blond-haired, blue-eyed young man of twenty-one, with a squat Germanic face. We conversed in German, as he knew no English, and when I told him I had shot him down he surprised me somewhat by seizing my hand and congratulating me. He did not know what had caused his aeroplane to do flick rolls, and was under the impression that we had collided. He was rather disappointed that he had not hit my machine at all. Apparently it was he who had tried to bounce us earlier in the fight. He was a Sudeten German who had Czech relatives, and said he was not a Nazi, but just became a fighter pilot for the fun of it! He told me that when he came down his parachute caught in the roof of a house and left him dangling just out of reach of a crowd of angry Maltese. He was rescued by some British soldiers. [13]

That was not the whole conversation. Johnny Johnston overheard their discussion, which included complaints from David about 109 pilots who machine-gunned RAF pilots parachuting or in dinghies. The German called such conduct 'Schweinerei' and would not accept that it had happened. He was told that a RAF pilot had been found in his dinghy shot with a cannon shell, and that the rescue launch had been attacked. He would not accept that this had happened. [14]

The position was not as wholly one-sided as David thought at the time. On 17 May Tony Holland was involved in a sortie he did not like:

> Johnny Hurst led Neville King, Pilot Officer Forster and me in an attack on the Dornier DO24 seaplane, heavily escorted by ME109s. We nearly got blown out

of the sky by the 109 escort, and were then chased back to Malta at sea level. We were all four lucky to get home intact and none of us could stay long enough to observe results. We had been ordered to attack, to prevent ditched enemy aircrew returning home to fight against us. [15]

It appeared that the RAF wished Axis pilots who had been shot down to survive as prisoners of war, and the Malta launch picked up no less that 123 RAF pilots, thirty-four German pilots, and twenty-one Italian pilots between mid-1940 and the end of 1942. The Luftwaffe on the other hand did not want Spitfire pilots to survive at all, whether they were flying, parachuting, in dinghies or being rescued on the launch. [16]

On 14 April the Malta Launch, escorted by three Hurricanes, had been attacked by ME109s, and was hit by six explosive cannon shells and twenty bullets. Similarly, on 18 May, the launch went out to save a Spitfire pilot and picked up a German pilot, who gave the advice that it would be wise to return to shore before the launch was damaged. They went on to pick up the Spitfire pilot first. [17]

All that Malta needed in mid-May was a constant supply of Spitfires to fend off the planned invasion. Considering the devastating losses suffered by the best parachutists in the German army in taking Crete, where they had complete Luftwaffe supremacy, the invasion of Malta would be far harder, with Spitfire pilots operating freely over Malta's airspace, and over the sea between Malta and Sicily.

At 6 p.m. on 18 May, six pilots of 603 Squadron were scrambled to escort sixteen Spitfires, which were arriving from HMS *Eagle,* nine of them coming to Takali, and two being flown to Hal Far. All of this was noticed in Italy and soon the Italian General Carboni, who was to command a Division in the Malta invasion, was openly expressing defeatist sentiments. [18]

In contrast David's utterances were full of resolve and his third letter to his wife gave a précis of the first three and a half weeks in Malta.

When I first arrived, and for the first two weeks, the raids were really terrific. At least three times a day, waves of Hun bombers would come in and plaster the aerodromes and harbour. They did an insignificant amount of damage compared to the effort they spent, and the losses they suffered.

The amazing thing was one could always get a grandstand view of it all from a nearby hill. It was an extraordinary sight. But once or twice, one had to be down in the thick of it all. Then the only thing to do was to seize a rifle and fire back, and one felt all right.

We have also had them at night, and once I had the house next door to where I was sleeping hit twice. But one never minds or thinks twice about it— I just stayed in my bed! However, it certainly gives one the will to fight back, and, to start with, the fighting was certainly very intense and we were hopelessly outnumberd.

But we hit back hard and with astonishingly small losses to ourselves. I have managed to destroy two ME109s so far (sharing one of them with another chap) and have also damaged another fairly well. I have probably also hit several other Huns but couldn't see.

I enclose a piece of the 109 I got all to myself— I shot the wing off in a head-on attack and the pilot baled out and is a prisoner (not a frightfully nice one at that, though he congratulated me warmly!) . . . It's all so much a new experience, and I feel it's most interesting to go through it all. [19]

Part of the interest of David's account of his interview with the German pilot lies in the fact that there came a time when such visits would be discouraged. 249 Squadron also tended to visit its victims, as its new Commander Laddie Lucas recalled.

On one occasion his Squadron dived fast and unseen out of the sun, through an unsuspecting screen of seventy or eighty fighters, towards the Italian bombers below. Lucas's section of four Spitfires, in a fast closing attack, disposed of the bomber to the left of the Victory formation of three. Most of the crew took to their parachutes as the aircraft, streaming flames, dived towards the coast out of control.

A few days later *[Lucas remembered]* three of us went to see the pilot and air gunner in hospital. As I approached a dark-skinned, strikingly good-looking Italian face looked up from the pillow; it was the eyes, pleading and plaintive, which caught my attention. Deliberately, as if to emphasise his unspoken message, he held up a heavily bandaged arm. The hand was missing.

Sickened, I turned away; I could neither look nor speak. The pathos was too disturbing. As we left the ward I had one thought only in my mind, never to let any pilot of 249 see another wounded prisoner again.

Air fighting till then had always seemed to me to be rather like a good game of Rugby football, with both sides coming together afterwards in a magnanimous blend of spirit. But this had finished all that. I had to force the incident from my mind.[20]

On 20 May the Chief of the Air Staff summed up the result of the Combined *Wasp-Eagle* operation. The return of the *Eagle* on 18 May had been so successful that the reinforcements had made a major contribution to the local air superiority. This was borne out by the casualty rate. At least sixty-four Axis aircraft had been destroyed, forty-five probably destroyed, and seventy-five damaged, whereas only fourteen RAF fighters had been destroyed and only sixteen damaged. Now the Luftwaffe were resorting to fighter sweeps with a small number of bombers, having given up heavy bombing raids for the time being.[21]

At about the same time General Ismay told the Prime Minister that he was making preparations to supply Malta with more Spitfires on 30 May and 6 June, and to send Spitfire engines and spare parts out by ship. Sixteen Beaufighters were to reinforce Malta, so as to safeguard the final approach of a convoy under heavy Axis air attack. Malta was to be used as a base to attack enemy aerodromes in Sicily as soon as the opportunity might arise.

For the rest of May relatively little happened, apart from the usual bombing raids. RAF Wellingtons or Wimpies, as they were called, bombed Catania in Sicily, and the pilots of 603 Squadron shot down several more Axis aircraft. The fighter pilots now came across a new hazard, the dysentery which was know on the island as "Malta Dog". With their inadequate diet most of the pilots went down with this disagreeable illness at one time or another.[22]

The bombing raids continued at night and the Spitfire pilots developed an admiration for the Beaufighter pilots based at Luqa. In April 1942, 89 Squadron, based in Egypt, had sent a flight of these night fighters under the command of Squadron Leader Paul Evans, DFC. Their aircraft were equipped with Mark VII (Air Interception) Radar, and a (Ground Control Interception) station was established on the coast of Malta, near St Paul's Bay.

The Beaufighters of Paul Evans were stationed in dispersal pens, spread out over many miles, which made it almost impossible for the German bombers to find them. The Beaufighter pilots started operating immediately.

In April and May they had many successes against the night raiders. The Artillery barrage did not penetrate above twelve to fifteen thousand feet, so the Axis bombers were tempted to fly above it. There they would meet the Beaufighter pilots, who by firing at them would force them to take evasive action, often causing them to fly into the anti-aircraft barrage.

The combination of the searchlights and anti-aircraft guns operating up to fifteen thousand feet, and the Beaufighters hovering in wait for high flying intruders, greatly discouraged German night raids.

The Beaufighter pilots served three months on duty at a time, Paul Evans having three such tours of duty in Malta. The role of the night fighter pilot and the Spitfire pilot were very different. The job of the Spitfire pilot was more dangerous, but the role of the Beaufighter pilot required considerable skill, landing at night on a bombed airfield with only two directional lights at either end of the runway.

Over the summer months of 1942 the Beaufighter pilots were so effective that the night attacks were reduced in number.[23] David watched these night bombings with fascination. There was a certain ghastly beauty about the barrage, resembling as it did a gigantic firework display:

The night raids were often very thrilling spectacles, although sometimes the nearby whistle of a bomb would make one curl up all tense in bed. Many flares would be dropped making one feel unpleasantly exposed if directly under them. Then perhaps a few High Explosives which showed up as a short puff of red flame. Sometimes I counted ten before I heard their whistle and crash. Incendiaries, too, were dropped in bunches, and these displayed all manner of coloured lights. They were all of the explosive variety and blew up after a few minutes.

All the time dozens of searchlights covered the whole island, forming cones at the raiders, and we saw many illuminations holding the raiders as they dived across the island.

The "flak" would produce little sparks of light all around the Huns, and as they dived the glowing red "cricket balls" from several Bofors guns would criss-cross in their direction. Once I saw a Beaufighter shoot down a raider—a small rapidly winking light for a second or two—then a small glow just in front of it, growing larger and larger as it circled downwards, and finally a splash of flame as the raider hit the water. It was a most revealing sight, and like the day bombing, rarely viewed from such close range.[24]

The arrival of even more Spitfires on 18 May, aided by the anti-aircraft Gunners, the Army, the Searchlight Batteries, and the Beaufighter pilots at night time, had confirmed the victory of 10 May. But now some of the Germans considered that perhaps there might be an easy way out for them. They could throttle the island into submission through certain starvation by the most rigorous blockade.

At the end of May more than ever the Maltese, the Soldiers and the Fighter Pilots in Malta depended on the Navy to bring food to save the Island fortress. Malta was living on borrowed time.

Chapter Eight

THE JUNE CONVOY AND INVASION POSTPONED

WHILE spare parts and light ammunition were taken to Malta by air and by submarine, the food needed to sustain the population could only be brought by convoy. Only part of the supplies of two ships had been salvaged from the March convoy, and there had been no convoys during April and May. Everyone in Malta yearned for the arrival of food supplies.

Whether it came from the east or west, any convoy would be attacked by sea and air from Italy, Sardinia, Sicily, Pantelleria, Crete and Libya, and even if any ships got through they might be sunk in harbour. So it was necessary for the fighter pilots to protect the harbour and its approaches for the arrival of the much hoped-for convoy.

On 1 June there was not a single raid all day. The respite in Axis air activity allowed some of the fighter pilots a few days off, and the opportunity to rest before the next period of intensive action. Each Squadron operated eight aircraft, and the flights of each Squadron took it in turns to go on readiness from midday one day, until midday the next. During this quieter spell every fifth day, one of the five Squadrons was stood down.

On these off-days the pilots could gain a picture of the country they were defending. One such day was the 2 June when Wing Commander Wells drove some fighter pilots, including David and six of the 603 pilots, to Ghain Tuffieha. They picked on a stretch of sand furthest from the hotel, but moved after seeing a couple of large unexploded sea-mines, one half buried in sand and the other lodged in the rocks. David gave an account of these more relaxed times:

The bathing was truly magnificent: the water was

beautifully blue and clear and, above all, not too cold. In parts it was almost tepid, and one could stay in indefinitely. Everybody got very brown from sunbathing.

For lunch we would go up to the local hotel, perhaps have a glass of Gozo wine. Unfortunately, the food shortage soon made it impossible to get any food at restaurants. Sometimes it was possible to arrange a sail in a dinghy, but this was more difficult, as so few whole ones were left after the "blitzes". At other times we would spend the day visiting friends in various parts of the island. It usually entailed a bicycle ride of a couple of hours or so, but hitch-hiking was generally easy as the few car-drivers were very sympathetic.

On one of these visits I came across two small English girls. The elder was about seven. On asking their history, I was amazed to learn that before the heavy raids started they had been evacuated from the London blitz to Malta of all places! Truly out of the frying pan into the fire! They had by now come to regard bombs as part of the normal run of life.

Other forms of entertainment included dances, still to be had in blitzed Valletta; cinemas, most of which showed very old films (when I was there "Ben Hur" was undergoing revival); and occasional variety shows. The best of these latter was given by a party called the "Raffians", composed of RAF personnel and girls working for headquarters (there were no WAAFs in Malta). They showed extremely good talent, and were often performing while bombs were bursting nearby.

The food tended to be a bit monotonous—Maconochie's tinned meat day after day—and there was never enough of it. Maconochie's meat became so much a part of our lives that the German "anti-personnel" bombs were nicknamed "Maconochie's Reply"! But for all that, we would have been very badly off had there not been a Mr Maconochie.

A delightful variety of fruit could be obtained: in midsummer there were figs, loquats, pears, melons and peaches. Tomatoes, too, were plentiful. Oranges and lemons came into season later in the autumn, but a few lemons could be had most of the year round. At first

111

eggs were easily obtained, and when we arrived we could usually have two for breakfast and two for tea, but this situation deteriorated considerably later. Rationing all round became very tight, and even bread was rationed. Most people soon lost a stone or more in weight.

However, we were very grateful for what blessings we had; for Malta, under siege conditions, was necessarily rather short of many of the comforts of life.[1]

In the evening, after the return from bathing, preparations were made for the arrival of thirty Spitfires for the five Spitfire Squadrons, two of them based at Takali, two at Luqa, and one at Hal Far. Of these thirty Spitfires, sixteen were expected at Takali, but only thirteen arrived in good condition. One crashed on landing, and two were shot down on their way, one off Pantelleria and the other off Gozo. Several of the Spitfires had Hydromatic airscrews, which the pilots regarded as a big improvement, since it gave the aeroplanes concerned a more rapid climb.[2]

On 5 June Malta had its first day of rain, which pelted down, giving relief after "the sweltering hot dusty days". There was no bombing and no operations all day, but this state of affairs did not last for long. On 6 June David led his Flight up to 24,000 feet and saw four or five bombers, surrounded by fighters. He dived on them squirting the port bomber and seeing strikes. A young Canadian Pilot Officer, Walter Macleod, also damaged the bomber, which began to smoke. Before they could make certain that they had shot the Savoia Marchetti 84 bomber into the sea, they were driven off by a large fighter escort, which shot up Macleod's Spitfire so badly that he could only just get back to Takali.[3] Pilot Officer Glazebrook damaged another bomber, but he too could not see if it came down.[4]

Each day something new was apt to happen. On 7 June it was a new type of German bomb. At 6 a.m. flares were dropped, but it was the crackers or butterfly bombs which interested the pilots most. These were dropped in containers which burst on impact, scattering hundreds of small grenades, each about the size of a cigarette tin. Some of them went off at once, and another type could be detonated by a lorry going over it. A Maltese who played with one at Takali was killed. The pilots found this new development more disagreeable than frightening.[5]

That day a telegram was sent from the Chiefs of Staff to the Commander-in-Chief in the Mediterranean, saying that "Malta cannot be allowed to surrender owing to lack of supplies without an effort being made to run the Eastern convoy. . . It is accepted that heavy losses may be incurred".

On 8 June David's Squadron suffered its fourth casualty, when Pilot Officer Barlow, from Rhodesia, was bounced by 109s. But despite its losses the RAF was growing stronger. The next morning thirty new Spitfires arrived, sixteen of them at Takali, and Malta was well reinforced for the arrival of the convoy.[6]

On 14 June Air Marshal Lloyd addressed the pilots. Two convoys were arriving, a large one from the east, and a smaller one from the west. Spitfires, Beaufighters and Beauforts had come to Malta to help protect the convoys. In particular some of the Spitfires were to be fitted with extra tanks and would patrol over the convoy arriving from the west, well over a hundred miles out from Malta.[7] Other Spitfires were to patrol the convoy when it came within sixty miles on the 15 June,[8] and David noted:

> By dawn on that day the western convoy was already within range of the island's aircraft. The air over and around Malta rapidly became thick with aircraft, and this continued until sunset. Sorties were continually being made by Spitfires, Beaufighters, torpedo-carrying and reconnaissance aircraft.
>
> The facts of the battle did not come out until later. The convoy had been very heavily attacked all the previous day when it came within range of enemy aircraft based on Sardinia and Western Sicily, and considerable damage had been done; but at the same time the convoy's guns and carrier-borne aircraft had exacted a heavy toll of Axis aeroplanes. On the 15th the attacks were again heavy, but not quite so continuous, and the long-range Spitfires proved a strong deterrent, bringing several raiders down.

Meanwhile, we received our first blow when the news came through that the largest convoy coming from the East had turned back. Nobody knew why, but it was evident that it had been severely handled in the bomb alley between Crete and Libya.

When the short-range Spitfires took over patrol of the western convoy in the afternoon, the attacks dropped off considerably. But the Huns had not quite finished. At dusk they sent out a force of fifteen unescorted bombers to attack the ships again. 249 Squadron were the lucky ones who intercepted that raid. About three 88s were shot down and others damaged, while the rest jettisoned their bombs and fled back to Sicily.

Our Squadron did over forty sorties that day but to our great disappointment we were able to fire no shots at all in defence of the convoy. Only one Hun was seen all day, and that was a lone JU88 in the distance. We could not leave the convoy to go after it, and it did no damage. No bombs were dropped on the island all day; in fact, no enemy aircraft even came over the island.

The island's aircraft destroyed at least fourteen Axis aircraft. Very few of our aircraft were lost— of the fighters only one Spitfire pilot. The Italian fleet too, had been battered, and several of their ships had been hit by torpedoes.

Towards dusk I flew over the convoy in the evening summer sunlight with the island in the background. I looked down and saw many little ships rippling their way through the water. There were no Huns about, and everything looked so peaceful, it was hard to believe that those ships had been through such hell earlier that day and during the whole of the previous day. Only tell-tale streaks of oil on the water behind some ships indicated that all of their journey might not have been so uneventful as it then appeared. In fact, there was not a ship that had not had several near-misses, and many had been damaged.[9]

The *Welshman* reached harbour ahead of the convoy, unloaded and sailed within a few hours. Of the six merchantmen which had set out from the west, two, the *Troileus* and the *Orari,* reached Grand Harbour. The other four, the British *Burdwan,* the Dutch *Tannibar,* and American *Chant* and *Kentucky,* had been sunk with all supplies, including 603 Squadron's baggage. More important, the tanker carrying petrol, had been sunk as well as two destroyers, and the cruiser, *Cairo;* three other destroyers and a minesweeper were damaged. [10]

In spite of the appalling cost, three ships had unloaded in Malta, but rationing on the island would continue to be very strict. The Governor, Lord Gort, said in a broadcast that the hoped-for supplies had not arrived, and "all possible savings in every commodity and stock" would have to be made. Food and petrol rations would have to be cut. The fighter pilots would have to walk a good mile to the dispersal hut on the aerodrome at Takali. [11]

Back in Britain, on 16 June, Winston Churchill reminded the Chiefs of Staff that the surrender of Malta would have a most heartening effect on the Italians and might bring them back into the war. This could not be contemplated, and every attempt must be made to relieve the fortress. The Admiralty were invited to put up a scheme for the largest possible convoy to go to Malta from the west in July, and the Air Ministry was invited to report on flying into Malta as much concentrated food as possible.

Churchill followed this up with a Personal Minute to the Foreign Secretary; "We are absolutely bound to save Malta in one way or the other . . . I am relying upon you to treat the whole question of the relief of Malta as vitally urgent, and to keep at it with the Admiralty till a solution is reached." [12]

Soon Churchill was in Washington, where he received a cypher message sent by General Ismay on 18 June. The message proposed that the President should be asked to lend the American oiler *Ohio,* due on the Clyde on the 20th, to carry fuel to Malta for the Spitfires. [13] Later on the 18th, Churchill sent a message to Lord Gort: "It is a great comfort to me to feel that you are in full control of this vital island fortress. You may be sure we will do every-thing to help you." Lord Gort replied thanking him, saying that the supplies of milk delivered by HMS *Welshman* had been very welcome.[14]

The Prime Minister was dismayed a few days later by the news that Tobruk had fallen, with 25,000 British soldiers taken prisoners. Ironically the setback had the effect of lessening the pressure on Malta. 601 City of London Squadron was sent on to Egypt to strengthen the RAF in the Middle East while the British Army was threatened.[15] David Douglas-Hamilton noted later:

> For the rest of June there were only about half a dozen visits by Italian bombers, but there was still the usual Hun fighter sweep every day. On one or two days not even fighters appeared. However, night raids increased both in size and frequency, and sometimes we had quite a nice little "blitz" of twenty to thirty bombers.
>
> The Italians, too, would try their hand at night, but they were usually satisfied if they dropped their bombs in the sea somewhere near the island. On one occasion they dropped them on the small rock called Filfla, just to the south of Malta. Their aim must have been good if they were aiming at the rock, but perhaps their navigation was not quite so good; for next day the Italian wireless came out with the news that their brave airmen had bombed the "marshalling yards of Filfla". The German night raiders, too, did remarkably little damage, even to civilian property, which was all they ever hit, although they dropped all types of bombs. The only trouble was one never knew where they would fall, and one night a stray bomb hit a billet, killing seven airmen. The Beaufighters continued to shoot them down almost every night, and sometimes we went up after them in Spitfires; but we never had any luck and only rarely saw anything.[16]

It was as well that there was a relative lull in the fighting. Late in June some of the pilots, including David, went down with "Malta Dog", which caused a number to be off duty for considerable periods. The remnants of 601 Squadron came to Takali as a third Squadron there.[17]

The reason for the relative lull was straightforward. Kesselring wanted the invasion of Malta to take place, and Hitler had scheduled it for mid-July. But having lost so many of their crack parachutists during the invasion of Crete, the German High Command did not have all that many paratroopers left. The Italians had enough paratroopers, but did not have the stomach for such an enterprise, believing Malta to be fortified like a hedgehog.[18]

One of their problems was that Malta was covered with stone walls, which meant that any forced landing by aircraft or glider would very likely lead to heavy casualties. This was a deterrent against a large-scale invasion by gliders. In any case, the walls surrounding the Maltese fields were constructed in such a way that a few machine-gunners could hold up a small army in its advance. Besides, after its defeat on 10 May, the Luftwaffe would not offer the same support it had provided to the invasion of Crete, and Malta had since been reinforced with many more Spitfires.

After the fall of Tobruk matters came to a head. Amid the resulting German euphoria Hitler and the German High Command had to decide whether Malta should be invaded, or whether the Afrika Korps should thrust forward to drive the British out of the Nile Delta. They lacked the resources to do both. Rommel sought Hitler's permission to chase the British 8th Army, and Goering, commanding the Luftwaffe, supported Rommel, fearing that Operation Hercules would be like the Invasion of Crete, with "gigantic" casualties and no certainty of success.

Field Marshal Kesselring on the other hand wanted the invasion to go ahead. He was convinced that the German High Command was thinking in terms of Continental warfare and did not fully understand the importance of Malta. He had wanted to go through with the invasion after the air attacks of April and May, believing Malta could be taken with a limited number of armed forces.

Kesselring was well aware that in June the Invasion Plan had been fully prepared. Two parachute divisions under General Student, one of which was the Italian 2nd Parachute Division, were preparing to sieze the southern heights behind Valletta, in an assault on the airfields. As soon as one aerodrome was taken, troop-carrying aircraft and aircraft carrying heavy weapons and tanks were to be available.

There would then be a feint attack against the bay at Marsa Scirocco, while the main assault by the Italian Navy would land two to three assault divisions just south of Valletta. These divisions would take the bombing with the help of the parachutists. All this would be preceded by the bombing of the aerodromes, the anti-aircraft guns, and the harbour and shore batteries. [19]

Hitler had his own doubts about the planned invasion, which he mentioned to his Staff. He felt that the Italians would not maintain sufficient secrecy, would lack the necessary warlike qualities, and might not arrive at the time planned to support German parachutists. Hitler held the Italian Navy in contempt, believing that it would not fight the British Navy, and might scuttle away leaving the German armed forces on Malta without help and supplies.

In short, Hitler was having many of the same doubts about Operation Hercules that he had had about Operation Sealion, the plan to invade the United Kingdom after the Battle of Britain. In each case the Luftwaffe had lost the struggle for the supremacy of the air.

Hitler believed that once Tobruk had fallen, supply ships could travel there via Crete, a much longer, more time-consuming and extravagant journey. On 24 June he made his fatal decision to overrule Kesselring, which helped seal the fate of the Afrika Korps. As a result at the key conference of Field Marshals at Sidi Barani on 26 June, it was made clear that Hitler wanted Rommel to take Cairo and Egypt, rather than risk the difficult operation against Malta. As Rommel was to thrust towards Egypt, the invasion of Malta was to be postponed. [20]

Thus it was that a small handful of fighter pilots, assisted by the Army, supplied by the Navy, and supported by the proud and determined Maltese people had undermined Hitler's resolve to invade Malta. Once the invasion was postponed, it would be difficult even for Kesselring to bring the subject back on to Hitler's agenda.

At the time that Hitler made his decision Air Marshal

Lloyd and the Governor of Malta, Lord Gort, arranged an Investiture for decorating a few of the airmen in front of the Castille in Valletta. Gort insisted that it be done in style.

Later Air Marshal Lloyd wrote of the event, which was held on 10 July 1942: "Facing us, at the bottom of the steps of the Castille, and awaiting the presentation of their medal ribbons, were the heroes of today and tomorrow, many of whom had fought in the battles between a David and Goliath." He mentioned in writing the names of some of the men from every part of the Commonwealth who had made the Investiture possible. These included David Douglas-Hamilton and his friend Laddie Lucas.[21]

Notwithstanding the fall of Tobruk, and the fact that enemies still surrounded Malta on every side, the island fortress was striking back. With Rommel advancing in Libya, his supply-lines would be longer, and the opportunity for Malta's torpedo-carrying Wellingtons, Liberators and submarines to sink his convoys would be greater. Malta was in fact retaliating with such deadly effect that the Germans would again try to "neutralise" her in the July blitz.

Chapter Nine

JULY BATTLES AND A REMARKABLE ESCAPE

DURING July 1942 the nature of the fighting changed. In earlier months the Spitfires had been so few in number that it was usual for them to attack Axis formations over Malta. Now that the RAF was stronger, the Spitfire pilots were sent out to smash the invading aircraft before they reached the coast.[1]

On 1 July, in an attempt to limit Malta's offensive role in sinking so many vessels supplying Rommel, the Germans sought to subdue the island by bombing. They attacked the aerodromes in strength, but now their raids, although continuous, were not on the scale they had been in April. Besides, their own losses were very heavy: and in the first ten days of July more than a hundred German aircraft were shot down, while Malta lost about a quarter of that number of pilots.[2]

David's Squadron had its share of the action. On 1 July the pilots in his Squadron were heavily outnumbered by more than thirty Axis fighters, but managed to shoot down one and probably a second, damaging many more. He noted in the Squadron Diary that six of his Squadron's pilots had had to save themselves by parachute since arrival in Malta.[3]

On 2 July Johnny Hurst did not return from a flight. David wrote:

Nobody saw what happened to him, but it was almost certain he was killed outright. He was a great loss to the Squadron. He had destroyed four and probably destroyed another six Huns. He was the first of the Squadron to be awarded the Distinguished Flying Cross in Malta, and it was sad that he never knew about it. He was a fine fighter pilot and used to take on enormous odds all on his own. After several combats, he had come down with his machine riddled with holes, but he had generally done much more damage to the enemy.[4]

Three rescue searches were carried out for Johnny Hurst but without success. That night at 1 a.m. a heavy blitz took place, including an attack on M'Dina. A heavy high explosive bomb went off near David, cracking the looking-glass in his bedroom, which he interpreted as a bad omen for the Germans.[5] On 3 July Beauforts and Wellington bombers successfully bombed a convoy of supplies intended for Rommel.

At this time the score of 249 Squadron was still mounting. Having been in Malta longer its score was well ahead of 603 Squadron, alongside which it operated "with splendid competitive accord". It was no ordinary Squadron. Many of the pilots of 249 were very experienced, and they shot down more enemy aircraft than any other RAF Squadron in the Second World War.

But it was not only experience which stood 249 in good stead, and David told a remarkable story.

They were now commanded by Laddie Lucas, an excellent leader and well-known in peace-time as an amateur golfer. One of their most recent acquisitions began to shine as an expert destroyer of enemy fighters. He was Sergeant George Beurling, commonly called "Screwball". He had arrived in June, and I had been offered the choice between him and another pilot for 603 Squadron.[6]

In fact, what occurred was a meeting between Laddie Lucas and David Douglas-Hamilton, after the arrival of a new batch of pilots from the *Eagle* on 9 June, when the pilots had to be allocated to different Squadrons. There was a suspicion on the island that Squadron Commanders in Britain, when told to nominate pilots for Malta, occasionally sent their less proficient or more difficult characters. It was unfair on the squadrons in Malta sweating it out in the Mediterranean sun, and often it was fatal for the nominees, who sometimes did not last more than a week.

Eventually the Air Ministry took action, but that day, looking at the pilots before them, Laddie Lucas and David Douglas-Hamilton did not know whom they might be choosing. They tossed a coin for the first choice. Little did they know that one or other of them would be choosing one of the greatest fighter pilots of all time. David lost the toss and Laddie Lucas picked George "Screwball" Beurling, a man with the instinct to kill anything in sight and the mind of quicksilver. David later confessed:

Someone (had) told me he thought "Screwball" was a rather crazy pilot and a line-shooter, for he claimed to have destroyed two FW190s on his first trip over France, which would have been good enough even for an experienced pilot. "Screwball" scarcely looked the part, wearing a lock of his long, sandy hair hanging over his brow. But beneath his brow he had a pair of steely blue eyes. He was generally smiling, and nearly always in what is popularly known as "good form".

It soon became clear that he virtually lived for aerial fighting, and had made a very deep and thorough study of the art. He once gave a lecture to all the Takali pilots, clearly demonstrating that he had thought out the finer points of shooting much more than any of the rest of us had. Needless to say, he was not asked to give this talk until he had established himself as an outstanding shot by destroying eight Huns in a very short time, and had completely convinced those who flew with him in action.

People who knew him said he would either get shot down early on or become an ace. He was certainly unconventional and up to the most amazing tricks. He was a brilliant pilot in every way, but it was his shooting that was most amazing. He did not just aim at the enemy aeroplane and fire a long burst, but aimed at one particular vital part of the Hun and gave a very short burst which generally brought it down.

I was completely convinced about him one day when he came down from a fight and claimed to have damaged a Macchi (he did not suggest he had destroyed it) with his two-machine-guns only, after his cannon had jammed, on the starboard side of the fuselage and in the port aileron. Some time later a report came through that a Macchi had crash-landed on Gozo with its ailerons jammed. It also had bullet strikes on the starboard side of the fuselage. No one else claimed it, and it could only have been "Screwball".

His score rapidly mounted during the July fighting, and by the end of the month he had brought his total up to eighteen destroyed, all of them fighters. Once or twice he brought down three in a day, and on another occasion got four in a day. He was slightly injured in the feet by a cannon splinter in one fight, but it did not put him off flying for a day.

He was terribly keen and could hardly wait to get up for a fight; there were invariably whoops of joy from him whenever the order to "scramble" came through. In another fight he was shot down, but uninjured; with two other pilots he had taken on a force of fifteen 109s. "Screwball" had destroyed one, and the other two had destroyed another and damaged a third before "Screwball" was shot up. Later in October he was again shot up and forced to bale out a second time, with slight injury. His parachute opened only about twenty feet above the water. By this time he had destroyed a total of twenty eight enemy aircraft.[7]

"Screwball" Beurling was without doubt a genius, but in Malta it was not so much the brilliance of the few, as the excellence of the many which played the greatest part in the struggle. For example, on 6 July the pilots of 603 Squadron, by acting as an integrated team had a very full day, dealing with the six raids on the island.

The Squadron was up for each of them, but did not have any luck until the afternoon. It then dealt with two 88 raids and one "Eyetie" raid in fairly rapid succession.

On the first of these at 4.20 p.m. we were sent up rather late, and had not got very high when the 88s came in and bombed Hal Far. We dived down on them, but just as we were drawing near them a number of 109s dived down on us. A terrific dog-fight ensued, in which the 109s for once stayed and fought. They were good those yellow-nosed 109s. We twisted and turned around each other, blazing away every now and then; but most of us could not get away to chase the 88s. Two of us, Pilot Officers Glen and Carlet, however, had eluded the 109s and chased the 88s right out to sea quite low down. They got one each.

Bill Douglas was shot up by a 109 and had to crash-land, but he was unhurt and anxious to get up again for the next raid. We had not long to wait.

The scramble order came at 6.30 p.m. about as soon as we had re-fuelled and re-armed, and once more we were climbing up, this time after an "Eyetie" raid. We were still too low when they dropped their bombs, but continued on upwards, keeping the "Eyeties" well in sight about five miles away. We chased them out to sea and shot up three of the bombers, with what result we could not stay to see, but one of us, Guy Carlet, destroyed a fighter. We all then "wizled" down and back to the island.[8]

It appears that David was more successful on this occasion than he realised. Tony Holland had said that:

He was very modest with his claims and would not permit himself or any of his pilots to claim a destroyed enemy aircraft, unless actually seen to hit the ground or water, and be witnessed by a second party either from the air or ground. As some of the scraps took place over water, surface witnesses were hard to get . . .[9]

This particular fight took place over the sea, and the Intelligence Records stated that Squadron Leader Winfield, Flight Sergeant Farquharson, Pilot Officer Glen, and Squadron Leader Douglas-Hamilton probably destroyed a Cant 1007 and damaged two Cant 1007s. The Operations Record Book also mentioned that David damaged a Macchi 202, so the chances are that he shot down more than he knew, and certainly even David could have had no doubt about the outcome of the last raid at 8.30 p.m.

He and the other pilots, 2nd Lieutenant Swales, Pilot

Officer Glen, Sergeant Irwin and Pilot Officer Carlet met three Junkers 88s and an ME109 just as they were coming into bomb to the north-west of Takali. Led by David, whose guns jammed after a few rounds, the pilots fired a few bursts head-on. They then followed David in a half roll and down in a dive after the German bombers, firing as they went. By the end of the exchange all four German aircraft had been destroyed. [10]

By the end of the day the Squadron had destroyed five 88s and two fighters, and damaged another seven enemy aircraft. We never had more than eight aircraft airborne, sometimes less, and suffered no casualties, although six of our aircraft had been shot up and damaged. It was the Squadron's best day in Malta and the island's best since the 10 May, for sixteen enemy planes had been destroyed and nineteen damaged.

The next day was the 7 July and the Squadron was not flying, but we saw one "Eyetie" bomber hit by a "flak". It streamed smoke, left the formation, and started circling down out of control and on fire, while a solitary parachute came out of it. Suddenly its petrol tanks exploded, and the big machine disintegrated into small pieces. Three more parachutes came out, but they all streamed, and their wretched charges were not long in hitting the ground. That must be an unpleasant death: one can see it coming inevitably a long time ahead, but there is absolutely nothing to be done about it.

A day or so later Neville King was lost during a battle. He had been flying with Flight Lieutenant Sanders, the Flight Commander who had succeeded John Buckstone, and early on they had both shot up a 109. The pair of them then chased some 88s out to sea past Gozo. Flight Lieutenant Sanders fired at one of them, but was hit by return fire in the middle of his bullet-proof windscreen. They then decided to return, but were very low on the water, and, in turning, Neville's wing touched the sea and he crashed.

Flight Lieutenant Sanders was then set upon by two 109s which chased him all over Gozo and finally shot him up so badly he had to come down in the sea. His aircraft stayed afloat just long enough for him to get out, and he was picked up by a fishing boat with no other injury than a black eye.[11] For once the Huns circled and did not shoot him up in the water. He went home shortly after that and Flying Officer Mitchell took over his flight.

The next day, 9 July, the Squadron shot down three or four enemy aircraft and damaged others, but the French pilot in the Squadron, Guy Carlet, did not return from a scramble. He was last seen diving on to an 88, and was presumably himself "bounced" by a 109. He had shown great promise, having destroyed three Huns on his first engagement.

After being badly shot up in the first ten days of July, the 88s gave up dive-bombing and took to high-level bombing. Apparently they found that dive-bombing, while producing better results, had left them too vulnerable. They had certainly lost a packet! Moreover, we soon learnt how to deal with high-level raids, and they began to lose as heavily as the dive-bombers.

Some days the Squadron had a great deal of bad luck about being sent off to intercept raids. One squadron had to be kept on the ground to deal with any raids following rapidly on the first one. However, these latter seldom materialised, and on two consecutive days (11 and 12 July) it led to our being bombed four times on the ground.

One or two aircraft were damaged, but no one was badly injured in spite of some narrow shaves. One party of airmen were in a slit trench when a bomb landed on the dispersal hut about three yards from them.

In another place a bomb landed close to a shelter in which were some Pilots; they were knocked over by the blast and had all the wind knocked out of them.

The same routine of readiness and off-time was being kept up, but owing to the intensified activity we did not have any squadron days-off for a few weeks at a time. That meant that everyone did about eight hours on from dawn till lunch-time, or from lunch-time till dusk every day.[12]

David's Squadron had by now lost seven pilots, who had come from all over the world. They were Pilot Officer Murray from the USA, Flight Lieutenant Buckstone from England, Pilot Officer Mitchell from New Zealand, Pilot Officer Barlow from Rhodesia, Flight Sergeant Hurst from England, Pilot Officer King from Ireland, and Pilot Officer Carlet from France.[13]

The death in action of friends can have an effect on morale, especially when men are driven to the limits of human endurance. David made his own assessment of the psychological effect of the battle on the pilots in his Squadron.

> We did not always get sent up even when a raid did come over, but whatever happened, most pilots were tired and generally felt like going to sleep after a spell of readiness. In the quieter days of June it had been the rule that most pilots on readiness read books. Now it seemed harder to concentrate on reading: we just sat round in the Dispersal Hut and waited. Some would chat with others and argue, but conversation was generally very mundane. Everybody concentrated on doing the job in hand—none knew what the morrow would bring—consequently there was little thought about the future. Most tended to be fatalistic, but at least we could console ourselves that the 88 crews must live in an even more profound atmosphere of fatalism!
>
> Some days a hot sirocco blew up from the south and nearly boiled us all. It made readiness periods very exhausting, and on our "off" periods we would lie down naked on our beds and swelter.[14]

On 13 July there were three raids, in the first of which eight Spitfires from 603 Squadron, led by David and Bill Douglas came across eighteen bombers in two waves of nine. They were met over the coast, and the return cross-fire was strong. The bombers were forced to jettison their bombs before reaching their targets, and several were destroyed or damaged. David shot up two Junkers 88s, damaging them, but again could not see what happened to them. Laddie Lucas, who had shot down six or seven

Axis aircraft over Malta, was shot up by three ME109s and crash-landed, but survived. After that the numbers in the raids decreased, and the raids themselves became more spasmodic. [15]

It was the last time that David fired at enemy aircraft over Malta, as he soon received promotion. On 20 July he became an acting Wing Commander and an Assistant Station Commander, with responsibility for making sure that bomb holes were dealt with effectively, in cooperation with the Army, keeping the aerodrome operational. Bill Douglas took over command of the Squadron. [16]

David's score had not been outstanding. He had shared an ME109 on 1 May, [17] shot one down on 15 May [18], probably shared in the destruction of a Savoia Marchetti 84 or Cant 1007 on 6 July, [19] and damaged some five other Axis aircraft—a 109 on 16 May, [20] a Cant 1007 on 6 June, [21] a Macchi 202 on 6 July, [22] and two Junkers 88 on 13 July. [23] He had fired at a great many other aircraft.

Tony Holland estimated that as damaged Axis aircraft had to cover sixty miles to reach Comiso and Catania in Sicily, it was reasonable to estimate that one-third did not complete their return journey. On the basis of this estimate David probably contributed to the shooting down of some four or five Axis aircraft, and Bill Douglas eight.

Of much more significance than his score was the leadership he gave to 603 Squadron. Wing Commander Jack Satchell wrote that David "was a born leader of men", [24] and Group Captain Cahill confirmed that he "was a great leader who inspired all under his command to do the almost impossible under rigorous active service conditions". [25] Tony Holland remembered him with affection as being reserved and pensive, when smoking his favourite curved pipe, and those who knew him well would readily recognise his appreciation of any humorous situation by the twinkle in his eye. His first concern had been for the well-being of the pilots in his Squadron.

Many of the pilots concerned, who had come from all over the world, had arrived with no operational experience, but within three months they had shot down forty-five Axis aircraft, with seventy-five damaged and fifteen others probably destroyed. [26] Seven of the pilots

David Douglas-Hamilton with his nephew Angus, later Duke of Hamilton, who twenty years after would follow his uncle into the RAF.
(Mrs. Brian Power)

26 March 1942: The SS Pampas burning in Grand Harbour after being bombed. It was one of only two ships in the convoy to reach Malta.
(Imperial War Museum)

Spitfire taking off from the USS Wasp on 20 April 1942, for the flight of 4 hours 10 minutes to Malta, 667 miles away. *(U.S. National Archives)*

After the bombing, Victory Street in Senglea lies shattered, every home and shop in ruins. *(Imperial War Museum)*

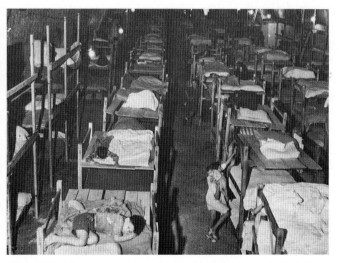

27 November 1941: A shelter hewn out of the rock, more than 100 feet below the surface, is filled with bunks for more than 1500 people. *(Imperial War Museum)*

Above left Air Vice Marshal Hugh Lloyd. *(Imperial War Museum)*

Above right Air Vice Marshal Sir Keith Park. *(RAF Museum)*

9 May 1942: The return of the USS Wasp, her hangar deck packed with British Spitfires. *(U.S. National Archives)*

10 May 1942, 5.35am: HMS Welshman reaches harbour, carrying anti-aircraft ammunition and spare parts for Spitfires. *(Imperial War Museum)*

Spitfire pilots led by Wing Commander Prosser Hanks scramble for action. *(Imperial War Museum)*

7 June 1942: 603 Squadron in Malta. At the centre is Squadron Leader David Douglas-Hamilton, with Flight Lieutenant Bill Douglas on his left.
(Mrs. Brian Power)

10 June 1942: A Bofors gun in action overlooking Grand Harbour.
(Imperial War Museum)

14 August 1942: The Brisbane Star with "a gaping torpedo hole in her bows" limps into harbour. *(Imperial War Museum)*

5 December 1942: The Lights of Victory, proclaiming the arrival of the United Nations convoy in Malta. At this time the Allies were referred to as the United Nations in Malta. *(Imperial War Museum)*

Above left 20 June 1943: King George VI visits the scenes of devastation in Valletta, Malta. *(Imperial War Museum)*

Above right General Montgomery in Malta, talking to Major Sym of the Seaforth Highlanders, just before the invasion of Sicily on 10 July 1943. *(Imperial War Museum)*

8 September 1943: Malta's moment of supreme triumph, when the Italian Fleet surrenders in Grand Harbour. Left to right: Marshall Badoglio, General Eisenhower, Admiral Cunningham, Field Marshal Lord Gort V.C., Field Marshal Alexander and Harold Macmillan, future Prime Minister of Great Britain. *(Miss Eliza Oxley)*

had been killed and four wounded, a low casualty rate, especially in view of the number of their missions and their previous lack of operational experience.

Overall the Spitfire squadrons were firmly in control. As David wrote:

By the end of July, 150 Axis aircraft had been destroyed, over a hundred by fighters and fifty by anti-aircraft guns. The renewed German bombing offensive had been defeated and virtually petered out. Not for one day had Malta's offensive power been affected.

At times, however, our fighter strength had been reduced to a dangerously low level by aircraft being shot up in the air, or damaged on the ground by bombing. Sometimes squadrons were reduced to two or three aircraft, but by the next day they were nearly always up to strength again. The maintenance personnel indeed worked wonders at repairing damaged aeroplanes.[27]

On 14 July Air Vice Marshal Lloyd received a posting and relinquished his command. Throughout the hardest times he had fought back by sending out his bombers. An unknown Maltese presented him with a cigarette case with MTAP on it, meaning "Malta thanks air protection".[28]

His successor, Air Vice Marshal Sir Keith Park, the veteran commander of 11 Group in the Battle of Britain, immediately insisted that Malta's offensive role must be sharpened and made more deadly. Enemy bombers must be shot down long before they reached Malta, and enemy aerodromes and bases would have to be attacked at the first opportunity.

He had come at a time when the RAF was growing steadily more powerful. Back in April Air Marshal Lloyd and Group Captain Woodhall had only been able to send three Spitfires and four Hurricanes into battle against more than 130 Axis aircraft. Now Air Vice Marshal Park was able to build on their success.

The Commander in Chief, Lord Gort, gave Park powerful support. On 27 July he wrote to the Prime

Minister, mentioning that with more than ten thousand homes destroyed by bombing, rehousing before winter would be a serious problem. He was filled with admiration for the Maltese who, though short of food, were showing "a stoical determination to withstand everything that it is humanly possible to endure, sooner than surrender to the despised Italians".

The steady reinforcement of the island with Spitfires had restored the morale of the Maltese, even if the average daily loss of Spitfires from various causes was about three a day. It was essential that Malta had enough Spitfires to cover the approach of a convoy, including the unloading of fuel in harbour.

A key problem was the lack of aviation spirit, and the dilemma for Lord Gort was that if Malta made a supreme effort without the necessary fuel supplies, she might exhaust herself in the process. On the other hand, if Malta remained content with defensive fighting until her stocks were restored, she could then play "an ever-increasing role in the final stages of the War"[29]. What he wrote would not be forgotten by the Prime Minister.

On the 29 July a curious incident took place, which must have its place in the Malta story. As David recalled:

A section of the Squadron led by Pilot Officer Dickie Sherwood were scrambled to intercept a mysterious single aircraft approaching the island at low altitude from the north.

A three-engined Italian seaplane, unescorted, was intercepted. Dickie could not make it out, but thinking it might be a torpedo-carrier after the ships in harbour, fired a burst at it and hit it in the wing. His No. 2 fired a burst across its bows, and it thereupon alighted on the water and stopped its engines about a mile offshore. Several people clambered out on to the wings and waved white shirts at the circling Spitfires. A launch then came and towed the seaplane into a bay. On telephoning up about it we were told it was a Cant 506 and that on board there were five hostile and four friendly persons in the crew. What could this mean? Italians deserting and overpowering part of their crew?

Eventually the whole story came out.

The four "friendly" were the crew of a Beaufort who had set out on a "strike" after enemy shipping the day before. *[The Captain was Lieutenant Strever from South Africa, and the other crew were Flying Officer Dunsmore from England, Sergeant Wilkinson and Sergeant Brown from New Zealand.]*[30] They located their target near Greece and released their torpedoes, but this Beaufort was damaged by "flak" and had to come down on the sea. The crew took to their dinghy. After a while they were picked up and taken to Corfu, where they were regaled by the the Italians and more or less fêted with wine and food.

Next morning they set out in the Cant for Italy with an Italian crew of five, including a pilot, a second pilot, an engineer, a wireless operator, observer, and a corporal who had never flown before acting as an armed guard. When they had been going for some time, at a given signal one of them *[Sergeant Wilkinson]* knocked out the guard and took his pistol, *[passing it to Lieutenant Strever,]* while the others *[Flying Officer Dunsmore and Sergeant Brown]* dealt with the rest of the crew. *[They used the corporal's body as a shield in approaching the first pilot.]* The pilot produced a pistol, but on seeing the determined look of *[Lieutenant Strever]* who had the guard's pistol, dropped it. *[Lieutenant Strever]* then took over control. They had some qualms about getting to Malta, because they did not know exactly where they were: they had no maps or charts on board, and they did not know if they had enough petrol. When Malta was mentioned to the Italian pilot, he threw up his hands in despair and said, "Too many Spitfires!"

In due course they saw Malta in the distance, and approached it low down. Just as they were nearing the island they had their most terrifying experience when the section of Spitfires *[from 603 Squadron]* attacked them. Control was promptly handed over to the Italian, and he was told to land. He did so, but had no sooner touched down than the aircraft ran out of petrol!

The Beaufort boys felt a bit ashamed at the way they had treated the Italians after the party they had had in Corfu, but decided that as war is war they had to do what they did. However, on landing they gave the Italians as good a party as Malta could provide. The Italian crew were just going on leave when caught, and had on their best uniforms and all their baggage with them. At the party in Malta one of them drew a bottle of Chianti from his case, and woefully exclaimed, "I had intended to use this quite otherwise!"

As a sequel, the Beaufort crew were all awarded the DFC and the Cant was forthwith utilised for Air Sea Rescue work. We had been wanting a seaplane for Air Sea Rescue for some time.[31]

Episodes such as this enthralled the defence forces in Malta, but the strain was telling on many of them. The *Welshman* had come and gone on 16 July,[32] and one ship could do but little to supply an island people. The food ration was so small that most pilots had by now lost two stone in weight. There was no doubt that the RAF were firmly in control, but the only worry of the Maltese and servicemen was that the convoy might not bring food in time. Everything now depended on the convoy lifeline.

Chapter Ten
THE CONVOY LIFELINE AND A FIGHTER OFFENSIVE

ON 1 August David learned that 603 Squadron had become the nucleus of the reconstituted 229 Squadron, partly because the ground crew which had embarked for Egypt in April 1942 had been unable to come to Malta by convoy, and also because seven of 603's pilots had been killed.

David was sad to leave his Squadron "after so many stirring days together",[1] but at least the pilots would be in good hands with Bill Douglas. On his departure from Takali David was sent on the compulsory leave for pilots to the RAF rest-camp in St. Paul's Bay. He described his experience there:

> It was the first leave I had had since arriving, and it was a pleasant change of surroundings. I spent every day lying in the sun and bathing off the rocks. There was also sailing to be had in small boats.
>
> I thought that here I should really be away from bombs for once, but in the middle of the first night I was woken up by two terrific bangs which shook the whole building. Some bombs had landed a few hundred yards away. A fine sort of "rest" camp, it seemed, if this was the ordinary run of affairs. However, it was only the usual erratic German night bombing, and did not occur again.[2]

David's new job involved working at Hal Far, from which many of the RAF bombers operated.

> Hal Far is the oldest aerodrome in Malta, and is situated at the south-east corner of the island not far from Kalafrana Bay. It once had a beautiful Officers' Mess, but one day a party of 87s made a dead set at it

and the Mess was no more.

Kalafrana Bay is an attractive spot and provides excellent bathing. There was a capsized ship, the *Breconshire,* in the middle of it, still visible above the waves—a relic of the March convoy. Divers were still managing to extract tins of milk and bottles of gin from it for months afterwards. It exuded oil and when the wind blew from the south bathing was rather unpleasant, as the water all round became impregnated with thick black oil. One of the sights of the bay was an 87 which was shot down and landed intact on the water in April. It sank in about twelve feet of water, and on a calm day could clearly be seen with the pilot still sitting in the cockpit. People said they could even read the time on his wrist-watch!

August began as a comparatively quiet month, though a fighter sweep of about twenty Huns and "Eyeties" came over most days, and occasionally an odd bomber or two as well. Very little damage was done, and the island lived in comparative peace.

Another convoy was due to arrive about the middle of August, and we were determined to do everything we could to get at least a substantial part of it through. In fact, it was to be a very large convoy coming from the west through the Straits of Gibraltar. Even more elaborate preparations were made than before, and fresh Spitfire reinforcements arrived from the aircraft carriers *Furious* and *Eagle, [led by Group Captain Walter Spencer Churchill, DSC, DFC, a kinsman of the Prime Minister, who would be in charge of fighter operations in Malta].*

As the convoy approached U-boats were sent to the western end of the Mediterranean. Mines were laid in the narrow waters, and many E-boats were brought into the area. At the same time hundreds of bomber, torpedo, and fighter aircraft were sent to the Western Sicilian aerodromes, to Sardinia, and to Pantelleria. The stage was set for a first-class battle.

The convoy passed through the Straits of Gibraltar, and on 11 August the *Eagle* was attacked by U-boats and sunk, just after a batch of Spitfires had taken off. A sad loss, but at least two U-boats were sunk in return. Then on the 12 August the fiercest day of the battle took place in the narrow waters off Tunis. The convoy was attacked incessantly all day by aircraft and E-boats. Several ships were sunk or damaged, but many enemy aircraft were also destroyed.

The next day the convoy was within range of Malta's fighters. First the Beaufighters, then the Spitfires, made sorties continually all day. Many battles took place, gradually decreasing as the ships neared Malta and came under the protection of our short-range fighters. The island's aircraft destroyed at least sixteen of the enemy. Again we lost very few aircraft.

Finally the moment came when one could sit on the cliffs and watch the ships coming in so bravely—those ships that meant so much to Malta. It was a most moving sight.

First, at 4.30 p.m. three merchantmen, the *Port Chalmers,* the *Melbourne Star* and the *Rochester Castle* came in escorted by destroyers.

Some hours later, early on 14 August, another big merchantman, the *Brisbane Star,* arrived. She came all alone, in reverse, with a gaping torpedo hole in her bows.

Meanwhile, the tanker *Ohio* from the USA, the precious tanker that was so vital to us, had been hit several times, a Stuka had even crashed on her deck, and finally bombs had smashed her engines. She lay stationary, some sixty miles from Malta. It seemed too ironical that that ship with its essential cargo should come so near after going through such trials, and yet be so far.

She was constantly patrolled by Spitfires which beat off all attempts to attack her, but nevertheless she lay there for about twenty hours, and it was not until next morning *[15 August]* that she was eventually towed in by destroyers *[strapped between them].* The fuel was all drawn off, and none too soon, for the damage had been altogether too great; and before long her back broke and she sank in harbour.

Her story was typical of the heroism which brought the convoy in. What a fight those sailors had had! But their efforts had borne fruit; for the convoy had ensured the life of Malta for another three months, and eased the acute shortage of supplies which had amounted to a crisis. At the time we only had enough petrol to last a fortnight.[3]

Beaufighters and Spitfires made 407 sorties once the convoy came within range, and these may have saved the five ships which got through out of the original fourteen. The Santa Maria convoy, as the Maltese called it, brought food and tilted the balance in favour of the island's survival.

The price paid by the Royal Navy and the merchantmen was severe. Nine merchant ships, the aircraft carrier *Eagle,* the anti-aircraft cruiser *Cairo,* the cruiser *Manchester,* and the destroyer *Foresight* lay at the bottom of the Mediterranean. The aircraft carrier *Indomitable,* and the cruisers *Nigeria* and *Kenya* were damaged as well at the battleship *Rodney,* and not one of the Merchantmen which had arrived was unscarred.[4]

Winston Churchill sent a letter to Stalin saying that now several ships of the convoy had got through, the fortress of Malta could hold out until after "the impending battle in the Western Desert". He summed up the frightful losses in these words: "I am of the opinion that the price was worth paying . . . The enemy will no doubt proclaim this as a great victory at sea, and so it would be but for the strategic significance of Malta in view of future plans".[5] Later, in his *History of the Second World War,* Churchill suggested that the Germans and Italians should have been able to destroy the entire convoy. But jealousy between the Axis powers proved helpful to the Allies. The Luftwaffe had insisted on attacking without the Italian Navy, and two of the Italian cruisers were torpedoed as they withdrew by British submarines. On 17 August Churchill telegraphed Admirals Syfret, Burrough and Lyster, congratulating them on "the magnificent crash-through of supplies to Malta".[6]

David noticed that "after this outstanding event the life of the island lapsed back into the normal run of Hun fighter sweeps. But no bomber attacks at all, by day or by night, were delivered on the ships in harbour".[7] Evidently past memories of attacking the harbour were too bitter. And the Germans were not going to be left to choose their own time for aerial activity.

Air Vice-Marshal Park, as Air Officer Commanding, was very offensive-minded, and at the first opportunity resolved to strike the Huns over their own territory instead of over Malta. Fighter sweeps were sent to Sicily sometimes with Hurricane bombers, manned by Fleet Air Arm pilots, accustomed to flying Swordfish torpedo aircraft. Rommel's convoys now made such wide detours around Malta that they were out of range of the Swordfish; consequently their pilots were almost "unemployed", and longed for something to do.

They had never flown Hurricanes before, but were given a few hours' practice in them and then sent over Sicily to "excite" the Hun, who showed remarkable reluctance to engage our fighter sweeps.[8]

On 19 August Lord Gort sent in a paper which was passed to the Prime Minister, outlining the terms of the new tactics and the adoption of "the forward plan", so that Axis aircraft would be intercepted over the sea between Malta and Sicily, before their bombers could reach Malta. "Casualties and damage to buildings, as well as to aerodromes and aircraft on the ground, have been very greatly reduced by this new method, and the effect on public morale has been most marked".[9]

It was not only the Spitfires and the Hurricanes who went over to the offensive. By the end of August there was so little business at night that the Beaufighters started night intruder operations over Sicily and the toe of Italy.[10]

But the more spectacular attacks were carried out by Spitfire pilots in day time. On one of these fighter sweeps on 27 August Air Vice Marshal Park sent three squadrons to execute an attack at low-level on the aerodromes of Gela, Biscara and Comiso in Sicily. Reports had been received of an increase in the number of Axis bombers there.

Wing Commander Arthur Donaldson, by then a battle-scarred and highly trained fighter leader, commanded the three Squadron Wing in the ensuing attack, with Group Captain Walter Spencer Churchill flying as his Number Two. Donaldson described the onslaught:

> We maintained complete RT silence so as to arrive unheralded. My Squadron was to attack Biscara. The flak was intense. I looked across at poor old Walter Churchill, and at that very moment he was shot down in flames crashing in the middle of the aerodrome. I saw a Dornier 219 bomber about to take off and by the time he was in my sights he was airborne. I chased him for about twenty miles. He had smoke pouring out of him and he was losing height, and disappeared below a small hill. I was not able to see him hit the ground, but it was obvious that he was a dead duck.[11]

During the raid at least ten Axis aircraft were shot down and twenty-nine were destroyed on the ground, for the loss of only two Spitfires. Arthur Donaldson received a Bar to his DFC for leading this highly successful attack.[12]

Towards the end of August, David was told tht he was to fly home, having completed his tour of duty, and was to take a message to the Air Ministry. Bill Douglas was to follow a short time later. David had just learned that he had become a father again, his second son being born only a few hours after the *Ohio* made harbour.[13]

David had formed a friendship with Arthur Donaldson, and on his final evening in Malta, before he was flown to Gibraltar in a Liberator, they had a round of drinks together.[14] Like David, Donaldson, who had arrived earlier in August, was keeping a Diary. Both men were Scots, familiar with and steeped in flying, but there was a difference between them. David was a passionately enthusiastic Volunteer and Arthur was an experienced, dedicated Regular Officer. Each of them had their part to play in the Malta Story.

*　　*　　*　　*　　*

In May 1942 the threat of invasion had been fought off by the fighter pilots and anti-aircraft gunners with the help of the Army. In June and August the spectre of starvation had been removed by the self-sacrifice of the Navy.

All this gave Malta the opportunity to recover and hit back. On 30 August a 5000-ton oil tanker was sunk by nine Beauforts and on 6 September further Beauforts from Malta sank a 10,000 ton motor vessel and beached another of 6000 tons. In September there were 124 sorties from Malta to attack Axis ships, forcing them to travel along the coast of Greece before crossing to Africa. [15]

Even so, the Luftwaffe still greatly outnumbered the RAF in aircraft, and a further confrontation on a large scale seemed inevitable. Kesselring knew that approximately one-third of the Luftwaffe in the Mediterranean, and virtually half of its total bomber strength, was based in Sicily, in order to cope with the threat to supply lines from Malta.

He resolved that an air operation must be launched against the island, to enable more convoys and supplies to get through to North Africa. Besides, if he managed to subdue and in large part destroy the RAF in Malta, he might possibly reopen the question of invasion before the forces were diverted elsewhere. [16]

In the meantime, Churchill, mindful that Malta was still short of fuel, drafted a Personal Minute on 13 September, saying "We must be careful not to ask Malta to do too much meanwhile, and General Alexander should be made aware of the fact that Malta cannot be run to a standstill". [17] This was followed up by the Chief of the Air Staff instructing Air Marshal Park to initiate all possible economies in the use of petrol. [18]

On the same day Lord Gort, as Governor and Commander-in-Chief in Malta, attended amidst the ruins of the Palace Square, Valletta, what can only be described as one of the most memorable ceremonies in the Second World War. He knew that King George VI had been desperately concerned at the terrible pounding from German bombers which the Maltese had been undergoing. The King felt as one with the Londoners when they had been involved in the Blitz, and on his own initiative he would give the Maltese the greatest honour within his power, in recognition of their fortitude.[19]

Lord Gort had waited four months, so that the ceremony of handing over the George Cross could be held in circumstances involving both the greatest safety and the maximum effect. On 15 September he sent in his own handwriting a Report to the King, concerning the significant duty which he had performed:

Sir,

Although I handed over the George Cross very soon after I arrived into the safe keeping of the Government of Malta, it was at that time out of the question to hold any big official ceremony at which a large crowd could be present. Recently we have had a quiet time and I decided it would be appropriate to hold the ceremony as near to Malta Day as possible. A weekday being out of the question, Sunday 13th September was chosen and an hour which would not interfere with any Church services. . .

I chose the Palace Square, Valletta, on account of its historical associations and the fact that it is so well known to visitors to Malta in peacetime. It has an especial interest as the Guard Room on the Square facing the Palace has written over it in Latin the following inscription to record the decision of the Treaty of Paris in 1814:

"To Great Britain, still unsubdued, these Islands are entrusted by the Powers of Europe at the wish of the Maltese themselves". . . . It has an appropriate ring about it today.

Shortage of petrol enabled us to control the size of the crowd as it was only possible to provide a skeleton omnibus service for the occasion. Even so between 4,000 and 5,000 people assembled in the Palace Square, many of them having walked long distances to be present.

As your Majesty will have learned, Sir George Borg the Chief Justice received the case containing the George Cross and Your Majesty's letter, on behalf of the peoples of Malta and her Dependencies. The case will now tour the villages of the Island and Gozo so that all the people may see it. . .

The people experienced the great moment of pride when Your Majesty first presented the George Cross to the Island Fortress and it proved to them that the aerial bombardments they had endured without faltering had earned for them an unique award from their King. At that time they were tired and weary but now that they have had a respite from bombing they are all the better able to appreciate the opportunity to see the George Cross for themselves in their own villages.

The arrival of the five ships of the convoy in the middle of August meant a great deal to us. It has permitted a small increase in the bread ration for male workers and a better issue of kerosene but, generally speaking, the additional supplies have enabled the Fortress to continue on the previous reduced scale of rations until early December. Aviation fuel and motor spirit both call for great care in expenditure if they are not to run out before the other commodities.

The people continue in good spirits and their loyalty to the British Crown remains unimpaired but, with the arrival of the autumn, we must anticipate a greater complexity in the problems which consistently confront us. It must always be the same in a beleaguered fortress and naturally the eyes of everyone in Malta are turned to the Middle East; a change of fortune in our favour in the Western Desert and an advance to Benghazi would permit supplies to reach us without the terrible hazards which convoys from the West entail.

I have the honour to be
  Sir
Your Majesty's obedient humble servant and subject
GORT[20]

As he wrote the RAF had more than one hundred fighter aircraft on the island. They were well serviced and when the Spitfire pilots took off in readiness for action, the chances were that their radios would work. Moreover when their cannons were fired, far from jamming as had happened so often in the past, the likelihood was that the cannon shells would streak their way across the sky towards their target.

Long gone were the days when Malta was down to its last six Spitfires. Through bitter experience the RAF had become stronger and highly professional, for if the war for the Mediterranean was to be won, before long the Luftwaffe in Sicily would have to be confronted.

Recently, disturbing Intelligence Reports had reached the Ministry of Defence in London, to the effect that if German aircraft could be withdrawn from the Russian Front or the Eastern Mediterranean, the Luftwaffe would undoubtedly try to neutralise Malta, to ease the Axis supply position.[21] A final reckoning was at hand.

Chapter Eleven

THE BREAKING OF THE LUFTWAFFE—OCTOBER 1942

BY early October the Germans were in a difficult position. Rommel's Afrika Korps needed more vehicles and military equipment. He would not be able to get them unless Malta was subdued. The Ministry of Defence in London knew that a large-scale attack by bombers was possible, but in their view its scale could not be sustained, so arrangements were made to reduce the number of British Infantry Battalions from three to one, and the number of Maltese Battalions from four to three.[1] It was not long before Kesselring's intentions became apparent to the Ministry of Defence, and to Wing Commander Donaldson.

On his arrival in Malta Donaldson had been put in charge of ground training, but he had soon been given command of the three Spitfire Squadrons based at Takali, numbers 229, 249 and 185. Like everyone else he was affected by the starvation diet, and he remembered his ration of fruit and nut chocolate being full of maggots. This did not stop anyone eating it. If it was good enough for the maggots, it was good enough for the pilots. Later on the pilots would boil the weevil-infested chocolate in water, skimming off the bugs, before drinking the rest. The only fuel for cooking came from oil taken from crashed aircraft, RAF and German alike. Consequently most dishes contained a fair element of sooty smuts.[2]

The grave shortage of food had required Lord Gort to take every step possible to reduce the number of mouths to feed. He ordered every aircraft which flew into Malta from either Egypt or Gibraltar to take out a complement of civilians who were contributing nothing to the war effort. No visiting aircraft could be refuelled from Malta's depleted stocks of petrol and this meant that the aircraft concerned could not carry much into Malta from Egypt as they also had to carry enough fuel to make the return journey. The occasional torpedo and a few sacks of dehydrated potatoes was often as much as the bomb bay of a Liberator could take.

The lack of fuel was further emphasised by the fact that the Spitfire pilots were forbidden to taxi their aircraft. All movement on the ground was by manpower only, the Army augmenting the RAF ground crews wherever possible. As soon as a Spitfire touched down, the engines would be switched off and it would freewheel or be pushed the rest of the way.

As there was only one runway at Luqa any aircraft which crashed on it and was stopping others from landing had to be unceremoniously dragged off by the one and only Cruisader tank left on the island. It was considered better to risk further damage to the one out of combat, than risk the rest running out of fuel in the air through waiting for the runway to be cleared.[3]

Relatively little had happened in September, apart from a few fighter sweeps over Italy. On 2 September Arthur Donaldson encountered a Macchi 202 and with two other pilots shot it down near Sicily. On another occasion he had engine trouble over Comiso, and glided back to Takali, an experience which before long would stand him in good stead.

He practised dropping 250lb bombs from his Spitfire, after an elementary bomb sight was fitted, and from time to time he dropped bombs on Sicilian airfields. On 11 October he was practising at Filfla, and after releasing the bombs, he noticed 229 Squadron taking off in haste. Kesselring's offensive had started, involving about six hundred aircraft. Donaldson joined 229 Squadron, which was one aircraft short. They saw three Junkers 88s, surrounded by twenty or thirty fighters. In the head-on attack which followed he destroyed one of the three bombers.

On 12 October the fighter escort for the German bombers was increased. Eight Junkers 88s came, accompanied by sixty to seventy fighters. This time Donaldson's wing surprised them near Sicily, long before they reached Malta. He managed to fly close in and this time definitely destroyed two Junkers 88s and one ME109. He also probably destroyed a Junkers 88 and another ME109. His description was of a scene which could not be forgotten.

It was the most spectacular sight I have ever seen. The whole sky was filled with enemy aircraft in severe trouble! I saw three flaming Junkers 88s and another three flaming ME109s, and counted no less than ten parachutes descending slowly, three of them from a Junkers 88 I had shot down. Two of my victims, a Junkers 88, and an ME109 both burst into flames.

This practice of forward interception could not prevent eighty people being killed on Malta and more than four hundred buildings being destroyed, but as a result a large number of Axis aircraft flying towards Malta never reached their destination. This required good controlling and accurate shooting at close range.[4]

The next day, the 13 October, Donaldson again attacked three Junkers 88s, surrounded by fighters, but his Spitfire was shot up and he was only able to make them jettison their bombs off target, landing safely back at Takali himself.

On 15 October, at 6.30a.m., the Luftwaffe launched one of their most powerful attacks. The Spitfire wing at Luqa had been scrambled, but made no contact. Arthur Donaldson scrambled with a section of three Spitfires, all that could be mustered at that moment, and they sighted eight Junkers 88s, with sixty to seventy ME109s. It was strangely appropriate that one of the last major battles over Malta should take place with four Spitfires flying into action, outnumbered by almost twenty to one, as the Gladiators had been at the beginning of the Air Battle for Malta.

As usual Donaldson led his section in a head-on attack, splitting up the bombers. He followed this up with an astern attack on a Junkers 88, but as he did so the two Spitfires behind him, perhaps because their pilots lacked experience, had been unable to follow, and there was no one to cover his rear against the 109s. Despite his vulnerable position, he pressed home the attack, getting his sights on the Junkers 88. As he fired, smoke and flames belched out of the bomber, but then it happened. Donaldson's Spitfire was riddled with shells, and the engine stopped dead.

He looked down, seeing blood everywhere, around his head, body, arms and legs, with petrol streaming into the cabin. He saw to his horror two of the fingers of his shattered left hand lying on his lap. With his good hand he found the controls, which seemed to respond, and he rolled his Spitfire over, diving downwards in order to make his escape.

As he dived he thought of parachuting, but ruled this out, thinking he might drown through loss of blood. He resolved to do what he had done in September, with engine trouble, and glide back to Takali. To his relief the ME109s did not follow.

As he reached Takali, where the aerodrome was covered with delayed-action and incendiary bombs, Donaldson made a belly-landing with wheels up. The firetender crew was on its way before his Spitfire had stopped, and regardless of the bombs strewn all around, he was pulled out of the aircraft and quickly taken up to Mtarfa Hospital, where his hand was operated upon.

During the following days, with the other wounded pilots, Donaldson watched the air battle from the verandah of Mtarfa Hospital. Everyday he saw the Spitfires tearing into the German bomber formation, and always the Luftwaffe losses appeared very much heavier.[5]

*   *   *   *   *

On the evening of 19 October the Luftwaffe sent in a fighter bomber formation which was met by Spitfires over the sea. While this preliminary battle proceeded, Kesselring sent in three large bomber formations from the North, the East and the West. A Squadron of Spitfires intercepted the bombers from the West, breaking up the formation over the sea, and then flew back over Malta, meeting the bombers from the East and shooting many of them out of the sky. With darkness coming on, the bomber formation from the North encountered a squadron of night fighters which prevented the vast majority of them from reaching the island.[6]

The next day there were only a few light raids over Malta and on 21 October the fighter pilots waited and watched for the Luftwaffe with their fighter escort. They waited and waited. Only gradually did it dawn on them that their terrible enemy had receded before their unbelieving eyes.[7]

In Sicily, Kesselring considered the results of the attack. During the period from 11 to 19 October the Spitfires had shot down about 131 Axis aircraft and had themselves lost only about thirteen pilots and thirty-four aircraft.[8] At the end of it Kesselring had called off the attack. As he later confessed, "Our losses were too high."

During the entire period not one aerodrome in Malta had been rendered unserviceable, and Malta's bombers consistently carried out attacks on shipping. There was only one night when the RAF was unable to carry out such attacks.[9] Fuel supplies for the Spitfires arrived in HMS *Welshman*.[10] The Luftwaffe had found the RAF stronger than ever before and its pilots no longer believed in their own invincibility. They had lost confidence, and were unenthusiastic about fighting a battle they knew they could no longer win.[11]

It was the last great battle over Malta, although skirmishing would continue spasmodically, and this time even Kesselring was forced to decide against pursuing the subject of invasion, "as the premises for success were just no longer there".[12]

While Kesselring nursed his humiliation, the New Zealander commanding the RAF in Malta, Air Vice Marshal Sir Keith Park, made his way to Mtarfa Hospital. He appeared at Arthur Donaldson's bed to inform him that he had won the Distinguished Service Order. Donaldson thus became the third of the only three brothers in the Armed Forces who all won the DSO; and all three had been Squadron Commanders in the RAF. His brother Jack had received the DSO before going down with the British aircraft carrier *Glorious*, sunk off Norway in

1940. In the same year his other brother, Teddy, received the award for leading a Hurricane Squadron in the Battle of France. Now Arthur had followed in their footsteps.

At the same time Lord Gort received a telegram of congratulations from the Prime Minister, Winston Churchill, which read:

> The work you are doing in animating the magnificent resistance of the island, and its effective intervention on the enemy's lines of communication, commands general admiration. Your name will be submitted to the King for promotion to the rank of Field Marshal in the New Year Honours List. [13]

With the assistance of the Maltese and of the defence forces, the fighter pilots had won the second great air victory of the War. They had done far more than save the island. By tying up such a large proportion of the Luftwaffe, they had enabled the British 8th Army to hold the Nile Delta. As General Playfair wrote in the official *History of the Second World War:* "Instead of starving Malta being saved by a victory in the Desert, it required all that the Island base could do to save Egypt." [14]

There was one man who knew this only too well. Shortly before El Alamein, a Canadian Beaufighter pilot was warming up the engine of his aircraft at first light, to take off for Malta, from the North African Desert. Suddenly a jeep drove up, and a General jumped out and walked over, displaying an air of enormous confidence. He told the Canadian Flight Lieutenant that he wanted him to give a personal message to Lord Gort at the Governor's Palace. After repeating the message, he twice asked if he had understood. The message was that Malta's heroics would make victory in the Western Desert possible . With victory in the Desert would go the liberation of Malta. The island would be saved. The Canadian pilot had been addressed by the Commander of the British 8th Army, General Montgomery. [15]

On 23 October two days after the defeat of the Luftwaffe between Malta and Sicily, General Montgomery's forces attacked in great strength, and gained victory at El Alamein. This was followed up on 30 October with Operation Supercharge. The timing of the attack was affected by the need to capture the Martuba aerodromes, so that air support could be given to the next convoy to Malta. The attack was a success, and soon the 8th Army was sweeping along the North African coast.

In Malta much of the population was still living in caves and shelters, and they all needed food. They believed that its coming by convoy would only be a matter of time, for they knew that the Air Battle for Malta had been won and El Alamein meant that its result was irreversible.

Chapter Twelve

THE RAISING OF THE SIEGE AND THE CALL OF DUTY

ON 8 November, as General Montgomery's forces fought their way from Egypt, a British-American invasion force commanded by General Eisenhower landed in French Morocco and Algiers. In order to assist the landings in North Africa, Malta-based Wellingtons flew from Luqa to drop bombs on Cagliari airfield in Sardinia. Every night there were sorties, and when the German intention to defend Tunis became apparent, Wellington bombers concentrated on bombing Tunis aerodrome, where the Axis transport and other aircraft operated.

Sicily also came under attack from Malta, with the Spitfire bombers dealing with Comiso and Gela airfields. Although on paper they were greatly outnumbered, resistance was weak.[1]

On 11 November Lord Gort informed the Secretary of State for the Colonies that the Council of Government in Malta were grateful to the British Government for a free and generous gift of £10 million, to assist them "to restore barbaric damage" inflicted by their enemies. They hoped that Malta would be "privileged to be the spearhead of the first thrust into Axis home territory".[2]

The gift had been Winston Churchill's proposal. Two months before he had written that the case of Malta was unique, and that "on account of the shattering damage, the Imperial Government should assume responsibility for building it up". It had not taken him long to obtain the agreement of the War Cabinet.[3]

The Maltese received further reassurance on 20 November, when the *Stoneage* convoy of four merchant ships, the cruiser *Euryalus* and ten destroyers reached Malta. They had set out from Egypt, had come under attack from torpedo bombers, and had fought their way through to Malta. Spitfires and Beaufighters had covered the last part of their approach, some of it in bad weather.[4]

In North Africa the thrust of the British 8th Army had made it possible for the Royal Air Force to operate from the Martuba airfields. When the convoy set out, it had fighter protection between Crete and Cyrenaica, an advantage which the June convoy did not have.[5]

As the ships came towards the Grand Harbour, the Maltese and the soldiers of the Garrison came out on the rooftops of Sliema, Senglea and Valletta to cheer, throwing caution to the winds. Overhead the Spitfires were patrolling, and there was not a sign of an enemy aircraft in the sky.

One of the Spitfire pilots watching was Wing Commander Sandy Johnstone, who had joined 602 (City of Glasgow) Squadron, when it had been commanded by David Douglas-Hamilton's oldest brother. During the Battle of Britain, Sandy Johnstone had commanded 602 Squadron and had had eight confirmed victories and at least four other probable victories. He had arrived in Malta, expecting to take over Arthur Donaldson's Wing, but Stan Grant had been appointed, so he worked as a Controller instead.

He saw the convoy entering the Grand Harbour and wrote:

> The Maltese went mad in a frenzied outburst of tears, laughter, and loud unrestrained cheering. Young boys and girls leaped and screamed, while their parents roared themselves hoarse as they watched the long-awaited convoy gliding in to safety. Old and young hugged and kissed each other; a few people just stood quietly, the tears of relief rolling unashamedly down their cheeks. Everywhere there were scenes of delirium. . . I have never seen such a heartfelt welcome being given to any force as was given to that small band of mariners who had opened up the sea route once again and given Malta the chance to breathe more easily.[6]

Two of the merchant ships flew the Stars and Stripes of the USA, one flying the Red Ensign was British and the fourth was Dutch. Within days 50,000 tons of stores and bombs and ammunition arrived. As well as these ships the the four merchant vessels of the August convoy, were also in the harbour, and as the unloading continued they all waited in readiness for a German air attack. But it never came.

Instead the Maltese had a small disappointment. Notwithstanding the convoy's supplies, there were still Axis forces in large numbers in both North Africa and Sicily. Malta would have to build up reserves, so for the time being rationing would have to continue.[7]

Now the Island had far more aircraft, taking off with bombs and torpedoes every day and night. At least five landing strips were operating, at Takali, Luqa, Hal Far, Krendi and the Safi strip, with aircraft dispersed in dispersal pens, sometimes one mile from the runway.

The activity at Takali had been scaled down, and that at Krendi had been increased in order to direct German attention away from the nearest military hospital at Mtarfa. Just before Christmas 1942, Sandy Johnstone was given the command of the Takali Wing, which was moved to Krendi aerodrome. As well as there being a great many aircraft, there was a force of destroyers with cruiser support to deal with the Italian Navy, and submarines were operating.

On 2 December four British destroyers, the *Jervis*, the *Javelin*, the *Kelvin* and the *Nubian*, which were based in Malta, were out on patrol. They saw an Italian destroyer east of Tunis, and once within range it was sunk within a few minutes.[8]

The RAF was equally active. The operations of the Beaufighters gradually spread to North Africa, where eventually night fighters were able to harass the retreating German armies. The Malta Night Fighter Unit of 89 Squadron, commanded by Wing Commander Paul Evans, had had only one loss over Malta. One of the Beaufighters had been shot down in error by the anti-aircraft batteries, but the crew managed to parachute to safety. Only two Beaufighters had been shot down on intruder operations, and they had destroyed a great many Axis aircraft.

Although slightly less manoeuvrable than Spitfires, with their very powerful armament, the Beaufighters now started to operate by day as well as by night. On 10 December, in bad weather, Beaufighters came across three enemy troop-carrying transport aircraft flying to North Africa. One of them was shot down, and on the next day a large number of German troop-carrying Junkers 52s were seen with a fighter escort.

Spitfires and Beaufighters attacked, the Spitfires dealing with the German fighters. The Beaufighters shot down six troop-carrying aircraft, with the Spitfires shooting down another two, a Junkers 88 bomber and four fighters. Many more were damaged, for the loss of only two RAF aircraft.[9] Air Vice Marshal Sir Keith Park was delighted and on 14 December he wrote to Arthur Donaldson:

Since you left, Malta has changed immensely, and we have for some weeks been carrying out an all-out night bombing and shipping offensive with five new Squadrons from Middle East, Krendi Strip has blossomed forth into a two-squadron station, and we expect the arrival of a Mosquito Squadron from UK shortly.

In fact, we have now doubled the number of Squadrons we had when you arrived here in August, and the Mediterranean Fleet and Convoys make the harbour look extremely busy. We have done everything possible to invite the enemy to blitz us again, but at the moment he seems to be too busy in Tunisia.

The Spit-bomber has been a great success, but our fighter sweeps rarely meet the enemy, though occasionally they slaughter an Air Transport Convoy trying to sneak past Malta, but well out of range of short-range fighters.[10]

In 1942 RAF fighters in Malta had destroyed 773 enemy aircraft, and had probably destroyed another three hundred, damaging many more. The anti-aircraft gunners had destroyed 182 Axis aircraft. The RAF had lost 195 aircraft and 106 pilots.[11] Park admitted that the results achieved by the RAF far exceeded anything imagined as being possible from the tiny island surrounded by enemies on all sides.

The RAF and the Royal Naval air squadrons, with the exception of a short period in April and May, maintained a continuous offensive, hitting 83 ships with bombs and torpedoes, and probably hitting another 52. The Axis losses inflicted by Malta-based submarines were also great.

The Navy had returned to Malta in strength, and on 21 December destroyers sunk a supply ship, while on 16 January 1943 an Italian merchant ship was sunk. The Navy's greatest success came on 19 and 20 January. On the 19th an Italian water tanker was sunk, and on the 20th two British destroyers met a convoy of twelve Axis ships. They sank eleven, and for humanitarian reasons left the last to pick up survivors.[12]

By this time the Spitfires had entered into their new role. In January 1943 Wing Commander Sandy Johnstone as the Wing Leader commanded the two Squadrons at Krendi, a runway perched alongside a cliff. He frequently led his squadron over Sicily, hoping to shoot Luftwaffe aircraft out of the sky, but they refused to venture forth to do battle. After experimenting with two 500 lb bombs fixed under the wings of each Spitfire, he learned that the plane could readily be transformed into a bomber.

For the first big raid on 16 January 1943 Johnstone led his two squadrons in an attack on a chemical factory at Pochino in Sicily. Twelve Spitfires each carried two bombs, with twelve more Spitfires acting as fighter escort. When they arrived in sight of the factory, the escorting Spitfires flew to one side, while each Spit-bomber made for the target.

In his book *Where No Angels Dwell*, Wing Commander Johnstone gives a gripping description of both the onslaught and his own emotions:

> In each Spitfire, with his 500 lb lethal weapon under each wing, the pilot kept his screaming dive under control while he zeroed the bombs on target by using the normal gunsight. One after the other the bombs

rained down on the target area, dropping at regular intervals and exploding with frightening velocity. At least three made direct hits on the factory, sending tons of masonry hurtling throught the air to join the twisted metal of the gutted machinery. As the last bomber began its dive I swooped down to ground level with my eleven escorting companions and raced in on the scene of destruction, raking the smoke and flames with cannon and machine-fire.

The vibration set up by the firing of the guns was like the tingling of newly awakened nerves. . . . It was a strange overwhelming feeling of excitement that made your mouth dry with the taste of it; your heart beat faster and your body tensed itself in its firm and unrelaxed grip.

Your hands gripped the controls as you put your fighter through its paces, and the quick responses to your demands seemed to mould you more firmly into the very heart of the machine until you were not merely there with it. When fighter and pilot were as one like this you felt invincible.

But it was a feeling which only took possession for a few fleeting moments when the thrill of the chase, the dog-fight, or the attack was at its height. Once it had ebbed away your brain told you once again that you were but a man—a mere microcosm of humanity—and that the fighter you flew was but a machine of nuts and bolts, of metal subject to all man's frailties. Back to reality you felt vulnerable; even lonely. . . .

I swept towards the wreckage of the factory . . . As I pulled back on the stick to lift the Spitfire above the smoke, there were clear indications that my fire power had struck home. There were signs of a large explosion and judging by the clouds of steam, followed by dense black smoke which billowed from the tall chimney and burst outwards from several of the factory windows, I was certain that I had hit a massive boiler.

Re-forming, the bomber aircraft, now shed of their loads, acted as escort to the twelve "straffers" whose ammunition was spent. We set course for Malta and were back on the ground, ready to refuel without any retaliation from the Sicilian-based enemy aircraft.

Back in the Island I discovered that owing to the speed which the bomb-carrying Spitfires had accumulated in their vertical dive on the factory, a number of seats had collapsed through the immense pull of gravity, exerted when they were pulled violently out of the dive. The pilots had been forced to crouch or adopt semi-standing positions in their cockpits throughout the entire flight back to base.[13]

This kind of attack had a marked effect on the morale of the fighter pilots and the Maltese. Indeed the RAF offensive was likened to the "flashing sword of Achilles".

The Luftwaffe was now concentrating on flying food and equipment to the Afrika Korps by Junkers 52 transports. Knowing their vulnerability to attack from Spitfires, they flew from Sicily to Tunis at sea level, below the radar screen. The Malta-based Spitfires were fitted with extra fuel tanks, enabling them to fly for up to five and a half hours, and they intercepted some of these transport aircraft. Not many got through to the Afrika Korps, which was now on the point of collapse.[14]

Meanwhile more supplies were reaching Malta all the time, and in March 1943 the siege came to an end when 40,000 tons were unloaded in Malta. The Maltese had lost more than 1,386 civilians in the 1,660 bombing attacks before the end of October 1942, and they had borne their ordeal with fortitude.[15] The Governor, Lord Gort, VC, paid a fitting tribute to the islanders, by quoting the words of General Monck:

"There is as much honour gained by suffering want patiently as by fighting valiantly, and as great achievements effected by one as by the other".[16]

As a result of the islanders' self-sacrifice, the dedication of the Malta garrison, and the advance of the Allies on 12 May, the Afrika Korps surrendered, and 291,000 Germans and Italians became prisoners of war. When the Maltese heard the news, the church bells started to ring, and there was dancing in the streets.[17]

On the next day, Air Marshal Park wrote to Sandy Johnstone, saying that Lynch of 249 Squadron, in the Krendi Wing, had shot down the thousandth Axis aircraft from Malta. Furthermore, Safi aerodrome had been completed and that week he would officially open it, flying off the first Spitfire, hoping that it would soon be the home of a Spitfire Wing.[18]

In April or May 1942 the small island might have fallen to an invasion force of a mere 35,000 men. Now its power to bomb and batter the Axis channels of communication meant that the Africa Korps could not be evacuated. Their supplies were cut off; and they knew that troop-carrying aircraft would be shot down. They had no option but to surrender.

In February 1941 Field Marshal Rommel had said: "Without Malta, the Axis will end by losing control of North Africa".[19] On 20 October 1942 Mussolini admitted that instead of Rommel's forces pressing on towards Egypt, it would have been better to take Malta. Rommel never made such an admission, but his papers include the ominous statement that "Malta has the lives of many thousands of German and Italian soldiers on its conscience". The Italian NID papers stated that "Malta was the rock on which our hopes in the Mediterranean foundered".[20]

It was appropriate that the man who had honoured the island most, in her darkest days, by awarding its people the George Cross, should visit Malta a few weeks after the siege was lifted. King George VI arrived on 20 June 1943 on the destroyer HMS *Aurora*, and when he came on to the balcony of the blitzed Palace in Valletta he received a tumultuous welcome from the crowds, men and women who gave expression to all their pent-up emotions as survivors of one of the most savage bombardments in history. The future British Prime Minister, Harold Macmillan, had been asked by the King to accompany him to the harbour, which was "packed solid with applauding humanity".[21]

Early in the morning the Roman Catholic priests had informed their congregations that the King was coming. Knowing that he was risking his life in coming at all, the Maltese and their clergy turned out in every square with flags, confetti and flowers. At first the King drove from one town to another, and later he visited the aerodromes, which had played such a big part in thwarting Hitler's Invasion Plans.

Leaving Malta, on his way to see the British 8th Army in North Africa, the King sent a reply to the Governor, Lord Gort:

> The warmth with which I have been received today has touched me more than I can say. It has been for me one further proof of the loyalty which has inspired the Island Fortress to withstand the fiercest blows that a cruel enemy could inflict on her.[22]

By early July 1943, the Royal Air Force had grown larger than ever before and almost six hundred aircraft were operating from Malta's five airfields and from the landing strip in Gozo, constructed by American engineers. Plans were being formulated in Malta for the use of air power to assist advancing troops on land. The island was about to become a launching pad for the invasion of Sicily.

On 9 July, the Seaforth Highlanders arrived in Malta, fully armed, and with them came some landing craft. It was noticed as well that the Supreme Allied Commander for Europe, General Eisenhower, and also the Commander of the British 8th Army, General Montgomery, were present in their new Headquarters in Valletta.

Some three thousand ships gathered that night on the North African coast and at Malta and awaited their orders. By morning they had left to invade Sicily, while a very large proportion of the six hundred aircraft on Malta provided protective cover and beat off enemy attacks.[23]

On 5 August, as the battle for Sicily raged, with British and Canadian forces fighting their way towards Mount Etna, General Eisenhower gave his own personal tribute:

The Epic of Malta is symbolic of the experience of the United Nations in the War. Malta has passed successively through the stages of woeful unpreparedness, tenacious endurance, intensive preparation and the initiation of a fierce offensive.

It is resolutely determined to maintain a rising crescendo of attack until the whole task is complete. For this inspiring example the United Nations will be forever indebted to Field Marshal Lord Gort, the Fighting Services under his Command and to every citizen of the heroic island.[24]

One person who had helped to give expression to the Maltese will to keep fighting was the Editor of *The Times of Malta*. She was the Hon. Mabel Strickland, and throughout the siege she had not failed to publish a single issue. On 17 August, after the fall of Sicily, she gave her opinion of the importance of the Battle of Malta.

The hideous German Junkers 88 no longer possess the sky, instead there is the continous drone of British fighters and bombers heading out for Italy, speeded on their mission by the Maltese with a fierce and furious delight. They are the first liberators of oppressed Europe.[25]

The frontiers of Fascism were steadily being rolled back, and on 3 September General Castellano of Italy signed the military terms of Surrender.[26]

On 8 September 1943 Malta had its supreme moment of triumph, when the Italian fleet, consisting of twenty-eight ships, steamed into the harbour to capitulate. In a fit of pique, the Luftwaffe had attacked and sunk the Italian battleship and flagship *Roma*, damaging other vessels. Now the bulk of the large and strong Italian fleet nestled within the waters of the small island it had once sought to subdue. On 28 September Marshal Badoglio signed the Surrender at Malta, in the presence of General Eisenhower, Lord Gort, VC, General Alexander, and Harold Macmillan. Admiral Sir Andrew Cunningham sent a telegram to the

Admiralty: "Pleased to inform their Lordships that the Italian battle fleet now lies at anchor under the guns of the fortress of Malta".[27]

The Battle of Malta was over and in November 1943 Prime Minister Winston Churchill visited the island. At the time he did not make any particularly glowing tribute to the Maltese and the Garrison, although he was well pleased with their success. As he saw it they had done their duty, and later he wrote his own verdict in the *History of the Second World War*:

> The Inter-relation between Malta and the Desert Operations was never so plain as in 1942, and the heroic defence of the Island in that year formed the keystone of the prolonged struggle for the maintenance of our position in Egypt and the Middle East.[28]

In contrast President Roosevelt of the United States, who had lent the USS *Wasp* to help save Malta, felt that the Maltese, the fighter pilots and bomber pilots, and the Garrison had done more than their duty. On Wednesday, 8 December he landed at Luqa aerodrome. Seated in his Jeep he was faced by the Governor, Lord Gort, Bishop Gonzi, the Service Chiefs, the Chief Justice, and the members of Malta's Executive Council. They were surrounded by the Guard of Honour.

President Roosevelt read out the terms of his own citation of honour, which was one of the finest tributes which could ever have been paid by a World Leader to the Island people and its armed services, after their long ordeal:

> In the name of the people of the United States of America I salute the Island of Malta, its people and defenders, who in the cause of freedom and justice and decency throughout the world have rendered valorous service far above and beyond the call of duty.
>
> Under repeated fire from the skies, Malta stood alone but unafraid in the centre of the sea, one tiny bright flame in the darkness, a beacon of hope for the clearer

days which have come.

Malta's bright story of human fortitude and courage will be read by posterity with wonder and gratitude throughout all the ages.

What was done in this Island maintains all highest traditions of gallant men and women who from the beginning of time have lived and died to preserve civilisation for all mankind.[29]

*　　*　　*　　*　　*

But what of those who had played a key role in securing Malta's survival? The war had to be seen through to the end, and as Lord Gort had said, there could be no glory without sacrifice.

Many ships had been sunk supplying Malta, and the three great ships which had done so much to save Malta, HMS *Eagle*, the USS *Wasp*, and HMS *Welshman*, had all been sunk. The *Wasp* was torpedoed on 15 September 1942 by a Japanese submarine, while covering reinforcements into Guadalcanal Island; HMS *Welshman* was sunk off Tobruk on 1 February 1943. In each case a proportion of their crews was saved.[30]

The Malta Brigade, consisting of the Devonshire Regiment, the Hampshire Regiment and the Dorsetshire Regiment, who had defended the aerodromes and coastline, now had to advance through Sicily and up through Italy, and sustained many casualties.[31]

Finally there remained the Spitfire pilots who had been at the sharp end of the battle throughout. Some were killed in accidents, and Arthur Donaldson was nearly one of these. The Liberator taking him to Gibraltar on 31 October 1942, overshot on landing and crashed into the sea while attempting to take off again. The Liberator broke its back, the bomb bay taking in water which flooded in as the aircraft sank. Donaldson saw a crack above his head and swam up through the broken hull to the surface. Six of the Spitfire pilots, including Eddie Glazebrook, who had joined 603 Squadron during its last days in Malta, were killed.[32]

The others survived, among them George Beurling

whose score of twenty-eight confirmed victories was the highest score of any RAF pilot in Malta, the Mediterranean, and North Africa. Arthur Donaldson had been fascinated to watch him off duty, practising deflection firing by shooting at lizards, aiming off when they were travelling fast, his actual hits being approximately ten out of ten. He was regarded as a genius, but by the end of his tour even he was suffering from war-weariness. He went back to Canada to lecture, and on 20 May 1948, by a cruel irony, he was killed in a bomber taking off from Rome Airport, while ferrying aircraft to Israel.[33]

A few survived. After a distinguished career Sandy Johnstone became the Air Vice Marshal commanding the RAF in Scotland and Northern Ireland. Arthur Donaldson was appointed Station Commander of the famous Battle of Britain aerodrome at Biggin Hill. Laddie Lucas took over the Spitfire wing at Coltishall: he arranged for Johnny Plagis and Bill Douglas to command two of the Spitfire squadrons, to complete a Malta Trinity.

Paul Evans the Beaufighter commander went on to command another intruder squadron working over Germany and German-occupied France. Later he commanded the RAF at Croydon, from which passenger flights began to take off for all over Europe.

Those who had served with David Douglas-Hamilton expected that he might be offered the command of a Spitfire Wing, but it was not to be. Tony Holland, who went on to collect two Distingusihed Flying Crosses, one from the RAF and one from the U.S. Air Force, had part of the rest of David's story.

Holland had been run over by a skidding lorry while on leave, and had broken a leg. In October 1942, David visited him in hospital. He was doing a ground tour as a Fighter Controller, but had volunteered for photo-reconnaissance duties where certain squadrons were being equipped with Mosquitoes.

The comradeship of commanding a Spitfire squadron could have been his for the asking, probably in Malta, where he thought that the battle had been won. David was exchanging this for the lonely and arduous task of acomplishing secret photo-reconnaissance missions over German-occupied Europe. The compensation was that, based in Britain, he might occasionally see his wife and his two sons, one of them newly born.

By October 1943 David was flying on secret missions with 544 Squadron. His navigator was a patriotic Englishman of Jewish origin, Philip Gatehouse, who had received a Distinguished Flying Medal for service in the Mediterranean.

Half of the pilots in the Squadron were killed, and David knew he was entering a high risk field, with the threat of anti-aircraft fire and enemy fighters always present. If he ran into serious trouble, he would have to weigh up the arguments and make his decision, trusting to luck.

The reconnaissance pilots were sent to places over the German heartland, with ugly-sounding names to them like Peenemunde, Swinemunde and Schweinfurt. One day early in August 1944 they were called in for their thirty-first mission. The Allies were going to invade Southern France, and they needed information about German fortifications, anti-aircraft positions, and aerodromes from Southern to Central France. This time they were asked to cover more targets than ever before, from Nice to St Dizier.[34]

At 10.15a.m. on 2 August, David Douglas-Hamilton and Philip Gatehouse set off from Benson, near Oxford for the longest mission of their lives. The hours ticked away. Five hours and twenty five minutes later, Leading Aircraftsman Brown was on Accident Card Duty, amongst others, on the apron of the runway at Benson Aerodrome, ready to put out fires and pull the crew clear in the event of any aircraft crashing.

As they waited a message was received from the Control Tower. Squadron Leader Lord David Douglas-Hamilton's Mosquito had reached the outskirts of Didcot, was within the circuit of the aerodrome, and was coming in to land, flying on only one engine. It had been shot up by anti-aircraft fire, and the navigator was believed to be seriously wounded and probably dead.[35]

One minute or so later they were told it was all over. The

remaining engine had suddenly stopped. The Mosquito was seen rapidly losing height, before it hit some trees and crashed.

As soon as the Mosquito was hit by anti-aircraft fire, seriously wounding, if not killing Philip Gatehouse, David must have known that parachuting out over the Allied Bridgehead in Normandy, or anywhere else, was out of the question. When one engine failed there was only one thing he could do—feather the airscrew, struggle on and hope that the other engine had not been damaged and would take the Mosquito back to a suitable friendly airfield.

The only question was which airfield he should select. There was Ford, a night fighter base near the Sussex coast, or Manston in Kent, with its exceptionally long and wide runway, or Benson itself. His Flight Plan provided for a return to base, and in any case, whatever the difficulties and dangers, he would have given priority to bringing back the photographs and fulfilling his mission, which for all he knew might be of the utmost importance to his country. His decision was similar to those he had taken so many times in Malta, to go on whatever the risks might be.

As their Mosquito came towards Benson, it "was seen by eye-witnesses to have the port wheel down, and in the process of being retracted".[36] The assumption must be that the hydraulics had been damaged, and that when he realised that the undercarriage would not operate properly, he had attempted to do a wheels up, belly landing.

Immediately after those on Accident Card duty had been stood down, a telephone call was made up to Dr Bevan Jones at Harwell research establishment, asking him to go to South Moreton Poultry Farm, to see if he could help the men in the crashed aircraft.

A few days before he had welcomed David at his home, and they had discussed the kind of world there would be after the end of the War. Dr Jones made his way to the farm, but had only to survey the scene, with the wreckage strewn all around, for a split second to know that there was nothing that could ever be done for the men who had crashed. He was shocked to learn that one of them was his friend. Even the photographs they had brought back were destroyed.[37]

A few minutes later David's wife Prunella arrived at Benson Aerodrome to meet him and was told what happened. Philip Gatehouse had been an only child, and his mother wrote to Prunella saying that they had been "a perfect team" and that: "We must take comfort, knowing they died as they would have wished, together, doing their duty".[38]

Meanwhile, the Operations Record Book had been written up, for once breaking out of its staccato style, saying that their loss was "a very serious one to the Squadron".[39] A young officer in the Flight, Squadron Leader Frank Dodd, was asked to step forward and take David's place. He was sent back to France to take pictures of some of the targets which David had been sent to photograph. This time the German anti-aircraft gunners did not succeed, and the Invasion of Southern France went ahead as planned, on 15 August 1944. It proved to be a complete success, hastening the liberation of France and the end of the War.

Nearly forty years on Frank Dodd had become a full Air Vice Marshal, with the Air Force Cross, the Distinguished Flying Cross, and the Distinguished Service Order, and he wrote about his predecessor in these words:

> David had the calm assurance of one who had looked death in the face and had not been afraid of what he saw. His presence somehow calmed any fears there may have been and raised morale when things looked grim. Others achieved results by a "charge and cheer" approach, but such was not his manner.[40]

It was ironical that having escaped death on countless occasions over the Mediterranean, David should end his life in an English field. Shortly before his death on operation, he had completed his notes giving his own estimate of why it was that the fighter pilots, with the support of the garrison and the Maltese, had won the second great air victory of the War. It reads strangely like the fighter pilot's epitaph on the Air Battle for Malta.

Part III

"Battle-scarred George Cross Malta
Stands Firm, undaunted and
undismayed, waiting for the time
when she can call:
    'Pass friend, all is well in the island
fortress!' "

Words of the Governor, Lord Gort VC
handing over the George Cross to the
Chief Justice Sir George Borg in the Palace
Square, Valletta, 13 September 1942

Chapter Thirteen

THE FIGHTER PILOTS AND
THE VICTORY OF MALTA

AT the beginning of the Battle of Malta, the Gladiator pilots, flying "Faith, Hope, and Charity", had led the resistance. One of these pilots, Wing Commander Burges, later said:

> My lasting impression of Malta at War is of an island whose strength was its unity and singleness of purpose. This produced an invincible defence and a formidable offence.[1]

When David arrived in April 1942, he was at once impressed with the extent of the teamwork and co-operation which existed in the Garrison. He wrote:

> In the account of experiences in Malta I have written from the point of view of a fighter pilot, and naturally that aspect has been stressed; but I do not wish in any way to minimise the work of the other Services and various Civil Defence organisations that kept Malta going. If I do not mention them it is merely because I did not come in contact with them so much.
>
> The fighters, of course, got most of the highlights of the Malta battle, but their job would have been impossible but for the untiring energy of others, especially of the RAF ground personnel. These men, many of whom had been in Malta for two years or more, put in sterling service the whole time. Compared with men in a similar job in this country, they had to work harder under much more trying circumstances. They were bombed frequently on the ground in the target area and suffered casualties, sometimes while the pilots were in the air or off duty. They had to walk a long way to and from their billets, and generally worked in the open air under the hot sun. At the same time they

were living on very short rations.

The difficulties of maintenance were great and many, and frequently the men were overburdened with aircraft requiring repair. But their vital work was carried out rapidly and efficiently, although they often had to improvise when spare parts were not available. An exceptionally high state of serviceability was maintained. They were always a cheery lot, and happiest when they were shooting at ME109s with a rifle or when their particular aeroplane landed having scored a victory or two.

Co-operation between the Services was extremely close, and founded on mutual respect. Discipline and morale were excellent throughout, and never was saluting more punctilious. Admiration for the Army was especially high in the RAF.

Throughout the whole of April 1942 the AA guns bore the brunt of the Hun attack day and night. The searchlights, too, played their part, and never have I seen so many illuminations of enemy aircraft as over Malta.

Whenever there was a bombing raid, however heavy, a party of soldiers stayed on the aerodrome, and as soon as it was over they were out filling in the bomb-holes. They were employed, too, in building blast pens for aircraft, and they even supplied armourers for our aeroplane crews. They really enjoyed working on the aircraft, and learnt the job in no time. Whenever there was any seemingly superhuman task of manual labour to be done, it was always the Army who did it. They were absolutely indispensable, and had it not been for them and their willing co-operation it would have been impossible to operate the Spitfires so successfully.

People often wonder how it is that Malta shot down so many Huns and "Eyeties", with such extraordinarily small loss in comparison. A similar thing happened on a larger scale in the Battle of Britain. Even on offensive sweeps over France, the Germans have been very far from reversing the figures. Indeed everywhere we have met the Germans on anything like equal terms, we have gained air superiority. So it is not solely due to the very great advantage of fighting over one's own territory, although that is an advantage which should not be minimised. Nor can it be solely due to superior technical efficiency on our part.

The Germans are excellent technicians and designers, and I am not one of those who believed the Spitfire V to be vastly superior to the contemporary Messerschmidt 109 (F). If it were it would be just too easy. All in all, in the hands of good pilots they are about equal, although personally I would rather fly a Spitfire every time. The key to the question seems to lie chiefly in the personnel.

The German bomber pilots were certainly highly disciplined and determined on the whole, and used to come in to bomb even when most or all of their comrades were shot down; but I cannot say the same of the German fighter pilots. Some of them were certainly very good, but usually they would not stay and "mix it" in a straight fight, and they always knew they were in for a fight if they stayed with our pilots. They would generally use the superior climbing powers of the 109 to comb away, sneak up behind us, and shoot when their victim was not looking. Maybe those are sound fighter tactics, but if they were in any way upset they would put their noses down and streak back for Sicily.

I remember an occasion when six of them were escorting a JU88 over Valletta harbour in the days when we were greatly outnumbered. One of our pilots shot the wing off their leader's plane, and the remaining five just "ran" for it— back to Sicily, leaving the 88s a sitting target, which the same pilot then dealt with. Had the Huns been really determined, none of us would have been able to land again safely in the days when relays of 109s kept us up circling base long after a bombing raid had passed.

No, the 109 pilot is at his best when he knows not only that he is in vastly superior numbers, but that he can shoot without his enemy being able to fight back; when he can shoot up a defenceless pilot dangling in his parachute or sitting in his dinghy or when he shoots up a harmless fishing-boat off Malta. Obviously they are the same Germans in both bombers and fighters, but the difference is in one of calling. The bomber pilot is given beforehand a definite task to carry out. The German is disciplined and brave, and like an automaton, does what he is told. But the fighter pilot is not forewarned of what he has to do. He has to seize opportunities rapidly, which the German's mind, dulled by over-regimentation, finds difficult. So he is at a disadvantage when up against our pilots.

One has only to reverse the position. If the Germans had held Malta in small numbers, and we had had large numbers attacking from Sicily, I do not believe the Germans would have stood it for long. They would have put up the white flag. If they had not, they would have had their fighter force wiped out in a few days, not by bombing on the ground, but by being shot down in aerial combat.

The Italians, on the other hand, have perhaps been rather too much maligned. They were not bad as fighter pilots, and their aeroplanes were certainly more manoeuvrable than 109s, and better able to turn and fight with our aircraft, though they lacked the performance of Spitfires. But the "Eyeties" were apt to do unpredictable and funny things which made everybody laugh at them. Their pilots, too, certainly had not got their hearts in the war like the Germans.

One of our leading air aces is reported once to have said that he had tried most forms of sport at one time or another, but that aerial fighting was the "king" of all sports. Though he undoubtedly did not mean the statement to be taken at its face value, there is nevertheless an element of truth in it. Through all the fear, emotion, and nervous strain of aerial combat there is an appeal in it that carries a challenge which few other warlike activities possess.

It is about the only form of warfare left in which one man meets another in individual combat, where the chances of success and survival to a large extent depend on the mental ability and physical skill of one of the two. Like a boxer before a fight, the fighter pilot lives on his nerves while he is on the ground at readiness, but once in the air he is a cold calculating force. He becomes a part of his machine and feels himself as such. He does not think of killing or wounding another man, but rather of destroying another machine which is out to destroy him.

Nowadays success in aerial fighting seems to depend much more on ability to fly well than it did in the last war. A pilot must be able to fly accurately, otherwise he will side-slip and his bullets will miss his target. "Screwball" Beurling, one of our "ace" fighter pilots, was certainly a firm believer in this, and I have seen few better exponents of the art of flying than he.

Naturally, it is not by any means all a matter of skill, and there is a considerable amount of luck in it, especially when engaging large numbers, or when, as happens to most pilots at some time, one gets shot at without knowing it. I was perhaps exceptionally lucky in this respect, for during the whole time I was in Malta I never had a single bullet-hole in my aircraft. I was the only one in my Squadron to have such luck.[2]

The was another reason for the victories of the fighter pilots. They had the absolute support not only of the Garrison, but of the Maltese people as well, many of whom had become anti-aircraft gunners, and this had a fundamental effect on their morale.

The Governor at the beginning of the Siege, General Dobbie, a Cromwellian figure, had worked ceaselessly and to the limit of his powers to protect the Maltese population from the countless bombs. He had also impressed the Maltese, who were deeply religious, with the fervour of his own faith and his quiet certainty that everything would come right in the end. He later wrote:

> The faith which many in Malta placed in God was, I think, the underlying reason of the fine spirit and courage shown by the people and Garrison, since many were receiving constant reminders that it is no vain thing to put one's trust in God.[3]

His successor, Field Marshal Lord Gort, VC, arrived in April 1942, when Malta was surrounded on all sides by a seemingly all-powerful enemy. It appeared that the end, either by invasion or starvation, might not be far away.

The Maltese were sorry to see General Dobbie depart, but Lord Gort soon became popular when they saw him bicycling his way through the debris and bomb damage of Valletta's streets, accepting their way of life as his own. They knew he understood what they were suffering. The fighter pilots too were encouraged when he appeared at the airfields before daylight, talking to the pilots as they were about to set off on their missions.

Very few men have held both the highest award for courage, as well as the most senior rank in the British Army: Lord Gort held both. He was not wholly dissimilar to La Valette, who had commanded the Malta Garrison in 1565, during the First Great Siege, and had given the Knights at St Elmo orders which meant quite literally that they had to fight until the last man was dead. Lord Gort, too, had about him the hallmark of a person who would fight to the very end, whatever the outcome and whatever the consequences. Not only that, he expected everyone else to do the same. He had the self-confidence of a man who was certain of his purpose.

When Gort handed over the George Cross to the Chief Justice, Sir George Borg, in the Palace Square, Valletta, he said: "Battle-scarred George Cross Malta stands firm, undaunted and undismayed, waiting for the time when she can call: 'Pass friend, all is well in the island fortress!'"[4] It is an awesome event when a leader of a Garrison, acting on behalf of his King, confers a great honour on a people, at a time when they do not know whether they will survive. At the end of the fighting those who do survive may find that they have won a greater victory than they had imagined possible at the outset.

The Malta story was an epic not only of the fighter pilots, but an epic shared to the full by the Garrison, the bomber pilots, the Navy and the Maltese people. It was also more than an epic. What they had done, through the activities of the three armed services, was to lay the foundation of the victory at El Alamein.

The RAF bomber pilots, the Fleet Air Arm pilots, and the submariners had destroyed ships in Axis convoys amounting to far more than 400,000 tons, with the result that Rommel and the Afrika Korps were starved of most necessary supplies. The war in North Africa had become a war of logistics, and by the time El Alamein took place the British 8th Army was attacking from a position of far greater strength. In the hands of an outstanding General, the outcome was a certainty before it began.

As General Montgomery had acknowledged, the Battle of El Alamein could not have taken place if Malta had fallen earlier in 1942. If the fighter pilots, assisted by the Army, had failed to stave off invasion, or if the Navy had been unable to fend off starvation by resupplying the island, or if the Maltese population had refused to support the Garrison, the Battle of El Alamein would never have taken place. Supplies would have reached Rommel and the Afrika Korps, for the most part unhindered: the Afrika Korps would rapidly have built up its strength, and would probably have seized the Nile Delta. Certainly the war for North Africa and the Middle East would have taken a different course.

But if the British 8th Army owed a debt of gratitude to Malta's part in the struggle, the Garrison in Malta too had cause to be thankful to those who had defended Crete with such valour in May 1941. During the fighting for Crete, the New Zealanders, Australians, British and Greeks made certain that the German victory would be so costly that Hitler would not risk sending German parachutists into Malta, in the absence of Luftwaffe supremacy. The invasion of Crete gave the Germans something of a Pyrrhic victory: it cost more than it was worth. Their losses made the Germans and Italians all the more anxious to obtain complete air supremacy over Malta's air space before invading.[5] When the Luftwaffe was defeated on 10 May 1942, the German invasion plans for Malta were thrown into disarray, and were never effectively resurrected.

It was left to the New Zealander, Air Vice Marshal Park, to avenge the fate of his countrymen, who had fought like heroes at Galatas in Crete until they were forced back by the overwhelming supremacy of the Luftwaffe and weight of numbers. In October 1942 the fighter pilots in Malta under Park's command effectively crushed the Luftwaffe in the confrontation over the Mediterranean.

The Maltese may have known little about the German concentration camps, but they were informed about the fighting elsewhere by *The Times of Malta*. They knew that the bombing and the planned invasion of Malta was a murderous affront to their religion and their way of life. Just how committed they were came home to one who wrote under the pseudonym "Bartimeus":

> I walked over a battery site, where for acres hardly a square yard of ground had not been blasted by the explosion of a bomb or was not part of a bomb crater: they fought with their guns here, cheering to hearten themselves. One crew, blown like leaves in all directions, picked themselves up and scrambled back to their gun, to find it buried at the bottom of a crater. Nearly all were wounded; but their immediate consideration was not the first-aid post; they set-to like badgers to dig their gun out again.
>
> They stood in a semi-circle round the gun, grinning like bashful children, while their commanding officer recounted the story. The lad who had been buried with his Lewis gun was one of them, a dark proud beautiful face like David going out against the Philistine in the Child's Bible.[6]

The Maltese felt that they were reliving the role of David fighting against Goliath, and that sums up the whole story of the epic Battle of Malta.

Today the last soldier, sailor and airman from the Commonwealth have long since left the island. Visitors can go to the Officers' Mess overlooking Takali aerodrome. It is now the Xara Palace Hotel,[7] with green fields stretched in front of it. In such a peaceful atmosphere, it is almost impossible to believe that this was a central point of the battle which raged for Malta, the Mediterranean, North Africa and the Middle East.

And yet there are two signs which confirm that the battle was no figment of the imagination. In Valletta's museum are the remains of a Spitfire of David Douglas-Hamilton's 603 Squadron. The aircraft was piloted by Flight Lieutenant Sanders and crashed off Gozo on the same day that Pilot Officer Neville King lost his life. It stands there as a symbol of resistance to the Third Reich and as a part of Malta's history which cannot be erased from the memory of mankind. Also in a beautiful spot on the hill of Bighi, above the harbour, are firs and cypresses. Underneath them rest the Spitfire pilots who fell in the battle.[8]

Theirs is a story which has been told since the beginning of time, the story of the sacrifice of youth for a great cause.

George Beurling as a fighter pilot stood head and shoulders above all other RAF fighter pilots in Malta. He had qualities of genius and E.C.R. Baker compiled the enclosed record of his astonishing achievements in his book "The Fighter Aces of the RAF". By the end of his term of duty, his score of Axis aircraft shot down was believed to be as high as 31 and one third, the latter being shared with two other pilots. This account is included in full, since no account of the Air Battle for Malta is complete, without a full description of his contribution to Malta's victory.

'SCREWBALL'

Squadron Leader G.F. Beurling
D.S.O., D.F.C., D.F.M. and Bar

AS as youngster George Frederick Beurling spent all his spare time watching aircraft at the airport a few miles from his home in Verdun, a suburb of Montreal in Canada. His father, a commercial artist, would have liked his son to train for his own profession, but after George's first flight in an aeroplane, when he was ten years old, there was no doubt as to what his future would be. Beurling wrote in his autobiography *Malta Spitfire*—"I was a flyer for the rest of time, no matter what happened." All his spare time and money were spent on flying lessons, and eventually he passed the flying and written examinations for his pilot's certificate—only to learn that he was then too young to be licensed.

The Second World War broke out and immediately young Beurling volunteered as a pilot in the Royal Canadian Air Force, but was told that his educational standard was insufficient to meet the extremely high standards of this service. Still determined to fly, George volunteered for the Finnish Air Force and was accepted, but his father refused to give his consent. Undismayed, George kept on flying and by the spring of 1940 had logged 250 hours solo flying. Wisely he also studied hard at academic subjects.

His next objective was to join the Royal Air Force. One day in May, 1940, he sailed to England, made his application at an R.A.F. Recruiting Centre and was told that he must produce his birth certificate. George did not have it, so back to Canada he sailed to fetch it. He returned to Britain on the same ship, working as a deckhand, produced the document to the recruiting officer and on September 7th, 1940, he was accepted for flying duties in the Royal Air Force.

From the time he enlisted Beurling's one and only ambition was to follow in the footsteps of the famous aces of the First World War. He trained with all his heart and soul, puzzled over the problems of aerial combat, absorbed all the knowledge possible, and when not on duty read and studied the life stories of Ball, McCudden, Mannock, Bishop and other ace pilots of the 1914-18 war. Every minute of his training period was devoted to making himself into a first-class fighter pilot. He excelled at shooting and each day would spend some considerable time at target practice, until he had become a magnificent marksman with all kinds of weapons and at all distances, both in the air and on the ground. He realised early on that keen eyesight was very important to a fighter pilot, and he spent hours on training his eyes to pick out tiny articles at great distances. He became so good at this that when he subsequently went into action he was nearly always the first member of his squadron to sight the enemy.

By December, 1941, Beurling had completed his training, which had been done under the expert guidance of that great Battle of Britain veteran, 'Ginger' Lacey, and was immediately posted to Number 403 Squadron. He took part in many fighter sweeps over the Channel and Northern France in the early part of 1942, but had to wait until May 1st before he shot down his first enemy plane, a Focke-Wulf 190 which exploded over Calais. Two days later Beurling repeated the feat. This proved to be his last victory in this theatre of war for some time, since shortly afterwards he was ordered to join Number 249 Squadron, which was stationed at Takali in Malta. This was already one of the crack Spitfire squadrons, having a total of 180 enemy planes to its credit, when Sergeant Beurling joined it on the 8th June, 1942.

Four days later Beurling had his first real taste of action in Malta, when he and three other pilots encountered fifteen Me. 109's. In a few minutes the enemy had been routed and were on their way back to their bases in Sicily, but not before young Beurling had badly damaged one of them.

'Screwball'—the nickname was given to him by the squadron, because he had a peculiar habit of calling everything and everyone by this unusual name—had to wait nearly a month after this before he had another chance to meet the Germans, for a spell of bad weather followed and the gallant defenders of Malta had a period of rest, whilst the bombers of the Luftwaffe and Regia Aeronautica were grounded in Sicily. On July 6th the lull ended and the enemy bombers started to raid the island again. Early in the morning eight Spitfires of 249 Squadron intercepted three Cant bombers and thirty fighters heading for Luqa. The Spitfires charged into the enemy formation, Beurling selecting one of the leading Huns as his target. He peppered its fuselage with cannon shells and machine-gun bullets, before he whizzed past and climbed to attack a Macchi 202, one of Italy's best fighters at this time. A slight touch on the gun button was all that was necessary to send the Italian fighter down towards the sea, burning furiously. Looking round, Screwball saw one of his comrades in trouble with a Macchi on his tail, so he swung across to help. The Italian dived away, closely followed by the Canadian. When the two planes pulled out of the dive 5,000 feet lower down Screwball fired a long burst of cannon shells. The Macchi broke up into small pieces to make Beurling's score two destroyed and one damaged in that fight. Returning to Takali, Screwball quickly refuelled and took off again to meet two Me. 109's heading for Malta. The Messerschmitts split up and tried to climb away, but Beurling was after one of them in a flash. He gave it a three-second burst after which it streamed a trail of white smoke until it dived into the Mediterranean Sea. The other Messerschmitt made off as quickly as possible in the direction of Sicily.

The Squadron was again up early on the 10th July to intercept four Junkers 88's escorted by about thirty Me. 109's. Beurling headed for the fighter escort and fastened on to a 109 which was about to open fire on a Spitfire. Screwball pulled up sharply under the tail of the Messerschmitt and fired into its belly. The enemy fighter turned completely over and then went straight down into the sea. On a second patrol later in the day Beurling found a solitary Spitfire being attacked by seven Macchi 202's. He dived into the middle of the fighters, scattering them in all directions. He followed one of them, which twisted away to escape the clutches of this fearless fighter, but Beurling stuck to it as if he were tied to it. For several minutes the combat went on, with Beurling just not able to keep the Macchi in his sights for more than a split second, until the Italian suddenly went into a loop. Beurling held off until it straightened out and then gave it a burst into the front of its fuselage. The next second the Italian pilot baled out. The rest of the enemy fighters had disappeared so Beurling joined up with the other Spitfire to fly back to Takali.

The next day Beurling and three other pilots met another group of bombers on their way to Malta. Again Sergeant Beurling attacked the fighter escort, this time diving on a Macchi and opening fire from a range of 300 yards. His aim must have been very accurate for immediately the Macchi fell away streaming glycol. As he closed in for another attack Beurling saw the cockpit cover of the Macchi slide back and then its pilot baled out. Ninety minutes later Beurling and another pilot on a second patrol found two more Macchi's. The Canadian caught up with the rearward of the pair, gave it a short burst and it went down in flames. Whipping round behind the other one, Screwball also gave this a short burst and it dived down to join its mate below the waves of the deep blue Mediterranean Sea. Two victories inside ten seconds brought Beurling's score to ten, eight of which he had destroyed in three days of fighting over Malta, which explains why he was awarded the Distinguished Flying Medal shortly afterwards for "displaying great skill and courage in the face of the enemy".

A fortnight later Beurling shot down four enemy fighters in a single day. On the early morning patrol, on the 27th July, the squadron intercepted seven Junkers 88's with an escort of about forty fighters. Screwball spotted a group of four Macchi 202's in line astern and headed for the nearest one. The Italian saw him coming and pulled away. Beurling tightened his turn and allowing for the deflection aimed in front of the Macchi. It flew right into the deadly stream of hot lead and next instant went down to crash-land on the beach near Kalafrana. In the meantime Beurling had caught the next Macchi, which exploded in mid-air. The other two Macchi's, their pilots thoroughly scared by the deadly marksmanship of the young Canadian ace, zoomed and skidded all over the sky in an attempt to avoid their pursuer, but they need not have worried, for Sergeant Beurling had already spotted two Me. 109's directly beneath him, and instead of pressing his attack on the Italians, he rolled and pulled up underneath the 109's. He caught the first one with a burst into the petrol tank and, as it went down in flames, used up the rest of his ammunition on its companion. Beurling then broke off the combat in order to refuel and rearm.

An hour or so later Beurling and three others climbed back into the battle to find twenty Me. 109's circling round four Junkers 88's. Beurling got on the tail of one of the Messerschmitt's and started to chase it round in ever diminishing circles, until the 109 finally stalled and fell away, with the determined Canadian hot on its heels. He opened fire, hit the Messerschmitt in the glycol tank, and a few moments later saw it dive vertically into the sea. This was Screwball's sixteenth confirmed kill. Not long after this Beurling shot down another

109, and was rewarded for his unbelievable run of victories by being awarded a Bar to his D.F.M. and a few days later was granted a commission.

During the next six or seven weeks there was a great lull in the fighting over Malta. The enemy stayed at home to lick their wounds after the enormous losses in the great air battles of June and July and only a very few bombers came over to try to bomb targets in Malta and these came mostly at night. During the same period the squadron's Spitfires were completely overhauled and there were also many changes in the personnel of the squadron. Squadron Leader Stan Grant, Flight Lieutenant 'Laddie' Lucas, and Flight Lieutenant 'Buck' McNair, who had been in the squadron for some time, were all decorated and then repatriated to the Mother Country. A new Station Commander, Wing Commander Donaldson, arrived and the squadron had a new Commanding Officer, Squadron Leader 'Timber' Woods, who had won his D.F.C. in the Battle of Britain.

Towards the end of September the lull ended and once more the Nazis sent over swarms of bombers and fighters in another attempt to wipe out the heroic defenders of Malta. But the Spitfires were ready for them and made the aggressors pay dearly for the attacks. Beurling and Flight Lieutenant Eric Hetherington by this time had formed a partnership which met with great success. The two of them would attack an enemy formation, pick out a victim, and Hetherington would make dummy attacks causing the enemy plane to come within range of Beurling's guns. A short burst from this expert marksman and he would be able to claim another victory. The Canadian was so good with his shooting that it was very rare for an enemy plane to escape once it had entered his sights. In this way Screwball soon became the top-scoring pilot on the Island and before the end of September had added the Distinguished Flying Cross to his decorations.

During the month of October Beurling was only in action for two days before he was repatriated, but in those two days he packed enough excitement to fill a lifetime. On the first of them, the 13th October, he was out with the squadron on the dawn patrol when they encountered fifteen Junkers 88's escorted by almost a hundred fighters. Immediately Timber Woods gave the order to attack and the Spitfires roared down in line abreast with guns blazing. Beurling fired at one of the bombers, but was himself attacked by about twenty Me. 109's, so he wheeled round and charged head-on into the group. He went straight through the Messerschmitts, banked steeply and came in directly astern of one of the 109's. He gave it a short burst, saw his shells striking the fuselage of the enemy fighter, and then the 109 exploded and fell to earth in small pieces. A slight turn now brought Beurling onto the tail of another 109, so he pressed the gun button once more. The cockpit hood of the enemy machine flew off and the German pilot baled out. The Canadian then turned his attention to the bombers, one of which he caught just as it was about to release its bombs. Beurling gave it a long deflection burst which caused black smoke to stream from its engines. Another short burst and the Junkers dived right into the ground. The rest of the enemy formation turned and fled towards Sicily before the resolute young airman had a chance to do any more damage.

The next day Screwball gave the Germans another lesson in marksmanship. It was his last day in action over Malta, but what a glorious day it turned out to be. Shortly after noon the whole squadron scrambled to meet eight Junkers 88's with an escort of about fifty Me.109's. As usual Beurling was off first and met the enemy formation just of the east coast of the island. He picked out a Junkers 88, gave it a two-second burst, and the raider, blazing from end to end, plunged headlong into the sea. At the same time a Spitfire shot past Beurling with eight Me. 109's on its tail. Beurling tore after the Huns and fired a long deflection shot into the leading 109, which immediately dived into the sea streaming smoke and shedding pieces. As the Canadian veered slightly to bring his sights to bear on another Messerschmitt, bullets and cannon shells from an enemy bomber tore into his cockpit and Beurling was hit in the hand and forearm. Yanking hurriedly on the control column, Screwball climbed quickly out of range of the bomber's guns and then saw another Spitfire in trouble below him. He went down vertically and pulled up underneath a Messerschmitt 109. He pressed the firing button as he closed rapidly on the German, saw the port wing of the 109 break away from the rest of the aircraft and then watched the remains of the fighter as it spiralled down into the sea.

It was a bad mistake.

He did not see the next 109 as it came in from astern, but he certainly knew it was there a split second later, when a hail of bullets and cannon shells smashed into his Spitfire. The controls were shot to pieces, and Screwball himself was hit in the leg, heel and arm, but he managed to struggle out of the cockpit and fall headlong into space. He pulled the ripcord of his parachute and thankfully breathed a sigh of relief as the large white mushroom billowed out above his head. He looked up and saw the Messerschmitt which had shot him down being chased by a Spitfire, and then he fell with a splash into the cool, blue waves of the Mediterranean. In a few minutes an Air/Sea Rescue launch picked him up and thirty minutes later he was in hospital, being treated for his wounds. He was still in hospital a week later when he heard that he had been awarded the Distinguished Service Order for his gallant action on the 14th October. He also heard, much to his annoyance and regret, that he was being taken off operational duties and being sent back to Canada.

Early in November he was flown back to his home country, where he received a tremendous reception, being hailed as the greatest Canadian ace since the days of Billy Bishop in the 1914-18 War. The Canadians now wanted him back in the Royal Canadian Air Force and in 1943 Beurling was transferred as a Flight Leutenant to Number 403 (R.C.A.F.) Squadron. He returned to operations with the squadron when it came to England, and on the 24th September, 1943, shot down a Focke-Wulf 190 during a sweep over Northern France. He shot down his last victim, another F.W. 190, over South-west Germany on the 30th December to bring his final score to thirty-one and a third confirmed victories. Soon after this he was taken off operations and spent the rest of the war as a gunnery instructor at Catfoss.

When the war ended Beurling decided to leave the Royal Canadian Air Force and for a time became a pilot with a civil air line in Canada. This was not exciting enough for Beurling and in May, 1948, he decided to join the Israeli Air Force, where he hoped once more to indulge in the art of aerial combat. His wish was never fulfilled for this remarkable man was killed in an air accident near Rome on the 20th May, 1948, whilst ferrying his aircraft to Israel. So died Screwball Beurling, the greatest fighter ace produced by Canada during the Second World War.

SOURCES

PART 1

1. THE STRUGGLE FOR SURVIVAL

1. Ian Hay, *The Unconquered Isle*, 1-62;
   George Hogan, *Malta: The Triumphant Years*, 20-24;
   Encyclopaedia Brittanica: History of Malta
2. Ian Hay, *The Unconquered Isle*, 84-5
3. Ministry of Information: *The Air Battle of Malta*, 11
4. Ibid, 12
5. Ian Hay, *The Unconquered Isle*, 90-91
   Stewart Perowne, *The Seige Within The Walls*, 42-45
6. Ministry of Information, *The Air Battle of Malta*, 15
7. Churchill, *The Second World War*, Vol. II, 443
8. Ibid, 400-1
9. Laddie Lucas, *Five Up*, 55-6
10. Churchill, *The Second World War*, Vol. II, 481
    Ciano's Diary, 305
11. Ministry of Information, *The Air Battle of Malta*, 21-5
12. Churchill, *The Second World War*, Vol. III, 54
    Public Record Office at Kew, PREM 3/266/10A
13. Ibid
14. Churchill, *The Second World War*, Vol. III 55-6
15. Public Record Office at Kew, PREM 3/266/10A
16. Walter Gorlitz, *The Memoirs of Field Marshal Keitel*, 142
    I. McD. G. Stewart, *The Struggle for Crete*, 8, 86
17. Ibid, 476-7
18. Public Record Office at Kew, PREM 3/266/10A
19. Ministry of Information: *The Air Battle of Malta*, 35-8
20. Ibid, 38-40
21. Churchill, Winston, *The Second World War*, Vol. III 492
    Ciano's Diary, 395
22. Ibid, 401
23. Churchill, Winston, *The Second World War*, Vol. III, 513
    Peter Shankland and Anthony Hunter: *Malta Convoy*, 39-40

2. HITLER, OPERATION HERCULES AND CHURCHILL

1. Ministry of Information: *The Air Battle of Malta*, 43
2. Ibid, 46
   Air Marshall Sir Hugh Lloyd: *Briefed to Attack*, 176, 179
3. Letter sent to the author by Group Captain Satchell D.S.O; dated 20:11:79
4. Ministry of Information: *The Air Battle of Malta*, 48
5. Public Record Office at Kew, PREM 3/266/10A
6. Ibid, PREM 3/266/2

7. Ciano's Diary, 461
    B.H. Liddell Hart, *The Rommel Papers*, 203
    Stewart Perowne, *The Siege within the Walls*, 128
    Peter Shankland and Anthony Hunter, *Malta Convoy*, 35-42
    Churchill, *The Second World War*, Vol. IV, 265-6, 271-2
8. Ministry of Information: *The Air Battle of Malta*, 48
9. Major R.T. Gilchrist: *Malta Strikes Back*, 6
10. Churchill, *The Second World War*, Vol. IV, 267-8
11. Ministry of Information, *The Air Battle of Malta*, 51-4
12. Public Record Office at Kew, AIR 20/914
13. Ibid, PREM 3/266/10A
14. Ibid, AIR 20/2428
15. Peter Shankland and Anthony Hunter, *Malta Convoy*, 53, 68
    Churchill, *The Second World War*, Vol. IV, 272-3
16. Public Record Office at Kew, PREM 3/266/1
17. Churchill, *The Second World War*, Vol. IV, 274
18. Public Record Office at Kew, PREM 3/266/1
19. Ibid, AIR 20/2428
20. Churchill, *The Second World War*, Vol. IV, 268-9
21. Ibid, 269
22. George Hogan: *Malta, The Triumphant Years*, 102
    The Times, 17th April, 1942
23. Ibid, 18 April 1942
24. *Tattered Battlements, A Malta Diary* by a Fighter Pilot, 71.
    The Author of this Diary was Johnny Johnston D.F.C.
25. *Blackwood's Magazine*, April 1944, 235
26. Churchill, *The Second World War*, Vol. IV, 273.

PART II

3. THE SQUADRON COMMANDER AND HIS DIARY

1. On 15 May, Air Chief Marshal Dowding, Commander-in-Chief of Fighter Command appeared before the Cabinet, to put the case that the bulk of Fighter Command be preserved for defence of the United Kingdom. What happened is well described by Robert Wright in *Dowding and the Battle of Britain*, 100-8. It was two days afterwards that Dowding sent Wing Commander the Duke of Hamilton to France to make contact with the R.A.F. Fighter Squadrons there, and to report back.
2. Papers of Mrs. Brian Power
3. Ibid
4. Public Record Office at Kew, AIR 27/2079
5. Papers of Mrs. Brian Power
6. Public Record Office at Kew, AIR 27/2079
7. Ibid
8. Francis Gerard; *Malta Magnificent*, 138
    Public Record Office at Kew, AIR 20/914
9. Ian Cameron; *Red Duster, White Ensign*, 109-113

10. 603 Squadron Diary 19:4:42
11. Stewart Perowne; *The Siege Within The Walls*, 119-122
12. Denis Barnham; *One Man's Window*, 38

4. THE FIRST USS WASP MALTA RELIEF FORCE

1. In a letter dated 19:11:1979 Tony Holland D.F.C. confirmed that
Sergeant Walcott shared a cabin with a Canadian pilot Flight Sergeant
Buckley to whom he let it be known that he had no intention of going
to Malta. Later in 1942 Tony Holland heard the rest of the story. After
belly landing the Spitfire on the South side of the Atlas Mountains, he
made his way to the nearest U.S. Consul, pretended to be a lost civil
pilot, and succeeded in getting himself repatriated.
2. *Tattered Battlements, A Malta Diary* by a Fighter Pilot, 74
3. *Blackwood's Magazine,* April 1944, 240
4. Air Marshal Sir Hugh Lloyd, *Briefed to Attack,* Chapters XIII and XIV
Public Record Office at Kew, PREM 3/266/4
5. Pilot Officers Paul Brennan and Ray Hesselyn; *Spitfires over Malta,* 43
6. *Tattered Battlements, A Malta Diary* by a Fighter Pilot, 79-84
7. Air Marshal Sir Hugh Lloyd, *Briefed to Attack,* 179
8. Ibid, 179
9. Public Record Office at Kew, AIR 20/2428

5. THE FIGHTER PILOT'S PARADISE

1. In a letter dated 17:4:80 Tony Holland gave this account.
2. *Blackwood's Magazine,* April 1944, 242-3
3. Ibid, 243
   603 Squadron Diary 21:4:42
4. Ibid, 22:4:42
   Blackwood's Magazine, April, 1944, 243
5. *Tattered Battlements, A Malta Diary* by a Fighter Pilot, 90
6. Account given by Wing Commander Paul Evans D.F.C., in October ,
   1980
7. 603 Squadron Diary
8. Public Record Office at Kew, PREM 3/266/4
9. Ibid, PREM 3/266/2
10. *Tattered Battlements, A Malta Diary* by a Fighter Pilot, 99-102
11. 603 Squadron Diary, 25:4;42
12. Pilot Officers Paul Brennan and Ray Hesselyn, *Spitfires over Malta,* 53-4
13. Ibid, 55
14. *Blackwood's Magazine,* April 1944, 243
15. Papers of Mrs. Brian Power
16. Public Record Office at Kew, PREM 3/266/4
17. *Blackwood's Magazine,* April 1944, 243-245
18. Ibid, 245
19. *Blackwood's Magazine,* May 1944, 370
20. *Tattered Battlements, A Malta Diary* by a Fighter Pilot, 116-7
    Pilot Officers Paul Brennan and Ray Hesselyn, *Spitfires over Malta,* 62

21. Letter from Tony Holland, dated 3:12:1979
22. *Tattered Battlements, A Malta Diary* by a Fighter Pilot, 110
23. Pilot Officers Paul Brennan and Ray Hesselyn, *Spitfires over Malta*, 64
24. Ministry of Information, *The Air Battle of Malta*, 64
    Air Marshall Sir Hugh Lloyd, *Briefed to Attack*, 162, 173
25. Pilot Officers Paul Brennan and Ray Hesselyn, *Spitfires over Malta*, 64
26. Ibid, 65
27. Public Record Office at Kew, PREM 3/266/1
28. *Tattered Battlements, A Malta Diary* by a Fighter Pilot, 117-122
29. J.R. Colville: *Man of Valour, Field Marshall Lord Gort V.C.*, 247-8
30. Pilot Officers Paul Brennan and Ray Hesselyn, *Spitfires over Malta*, 65-66
31. *Blackwood's Magazine*, May 1944, 369
32. *Royal Naval Biography*, Vol. I, 449
    The Memoirs of Lord Ismay 273
33. Captain S.W. Roskill: *History of the Second World War* Vol. II, *The War at Sea*, 66
34. Public Record Office at Kew PREM 3/266/2
35. Churchill, *The Second World War*, Vol. IV, 273

6. THE VICTORY OF 10th MAY

1. B.H. Liddell Hart: *The Rommel Papers*, 120, 203
   Stewart Perowne: *The Siege Within The Walls*, 128-134, 146
   Memoirs of Field Marshall Kesselring, 122-124
2. B.H. Liddell Hart: *The Rommel Papers*, 203
3. Memoirs of Field Marshal Kesselring, 122
4. Information sent by Department of the Navy, U.S. Historical Center, Washington Navy Yard, U.S.A. 29:5:1980
5. Letter sent by Tony Holland, dated 19:11:1979
6. *Blackwood's Magazine*, May 1944, 370
7. Letter sent by Tony Holland, dated 17:4:1980
8. *Blackwood's Magazine*, May 1944, 370
9. Ministry of Information: *The Air Battle of Malta*, 67
10. *Blackwood's Magazine*, May 1944, 371
    603 Squadron Diary 10:5:1942
11. Ministry of Information: *The Air Battle of Malta*, 70-1
    Blackwood's Magazine, May 1944, 371
    It should be noted that in the Ministry of Information publication, Flying Officer Mitchell was not positively identified. However, it is clear from the evidence in the Ministry of Information publication, in the 603 Squadron Diary and in David Douglas-Hamilton's account, that he was the pilot involved, since all three accounts correspond exactly in time, activity, position and effect, and he is identified in the other two documents.
12. *Blackwood's Magazine*, May 1944, 372
13. Pilot Officers Paul Brennan and Ray Hesselyn, *Spitfires over Malta*, 72
14. Ibid
    Ciano's Diary, 469

15. Pilot Officers Paul Brennan and Ray Hesselyn, *Spitfires over Malta*, 72
16. *The Times of Malta*, 11 May 1942
17. Public Record Office at Kew, PREM 3/266/4
18. Papers of Mrs. Brian Power
19. Memoirs of Field Marshal Kesselring, 122
20. Pilot Officers Paul Brennan and Ray Hesselyn, *Spitfires over Malta*, 7
21. *Tattered Battlements, A Malta Diary* by a Fighter Pilot, 65-70
22. Air Marshal Sir Hugh Lloyd, *Briefed to Attack*, 187

7. FEROCIOUS ENCOUNTERS

1. Ciano's Diary, 469, 475, 482-3
2. Ibid 469
3. *Blackwood's Magazine*, May 1944, 372
4. 603 Squadron Diary, 11 May, 1942
5. Pilot Officers Paul Brennan and Ray Hesselyn, *Spitfires over Malta*, 76-7
6. 603 Squadron diary, 12 May 1942
   Tattered Battlements, A Malta Diary by a Fighter Pilot, 59
7. Pilot Officers Paul Brennan and Ray Hesselyn, *Spitfires over Malta*, 82-3
8. *Blackwood's Magazine*, May 1944, 372-3
9. Ibid, 373-4
10. 603 Squadron Diary, 15:5:1942
11. *Tattered Battlements, A Malta Diary* by a Fighter Pilot, 128-9
    Blackwood's Magazine, May 1944, 374
12. 603 Squadron Diary, 16:5:1942
13. *Blackwood's Magazine*, May 1944, 374
14. *Tattered Battlements, A Malta Diary* by a Fighter Pilot, 128-9
15. Letter from Tony Holland dated 18:12:1979. He later found it ironical that on the same day his brother and Wing Commander Clarke were found dead in Cornwall being washed ashore after being involved in a shipping strike off the Channel Islands.
    603 Squadron Diary 17:5:1942
16. Leslie Oliver: Malta Besieged, 29
    Ian Hay, *The Unconquered Isle*, 172
17. Ministry of Information: *The Air Battle of Malta*, 75-6
18. Ciano's Diary, 475, 482
19. Papers of Mrs. Brian Power
20. Letter from Laddie Lucas dated 7 August, 1980
21. Public Record Office at Kew, PREM 3/266/4
22. 603 Squadron Diary, 27:5:1942
23. Letters from Wing Commander Paul Evans dated 15:9:1980 and 17:12:1980
24. *Blackwood's Magazine*, May 1944, 374

8. THE JUNE CONVOY AND INVASION POSTPONED

1. *Blackwood's Magazine*, May 1944, 375-6
2. 603 Squadron Diary 3:6:1942

3. Leslie Hunt, *Twenty One Squadrons, The History of the Royal Air Force 1925-1957, 107*
   603 Squadron Diary, 6:6:1942
   E.C.R. Baker, The Fighter Aces of the RAF 1939-1945, 139-140
   Wally Macleod, shot down 13 Axis Aircraft over Malta after this lucky escape, and went on to shoot down 21 Axis aircraft, before his death in action on 27th September 1944. He was one of the top scoring Canadian pilots in the Second World War
4. 603 Squadron Diary 6:6:1942
5. Ibid, 7:6:1942
6. Ibid, 8:6:1942 and 9:6:1942
7. Ibid, 14:6:1942
8. Ibid, 15:6:1942
9. *Blackwood's Magazine*, May 1944, 377
10. Captain S.W. Roskill, *History of the Second World War, The War at Sea*, Vol. II, 67
11. *Blackwood's Magazine*, May 1944, 377
12. Public Record Office at Kew, PREM 3/266/2
13. Ibid, PREM 3/266/2
14. Ibid, PREM 3/266/2
15. 603 Squadron Diary, 21:6:1942
16. *Blackwood's Magazine*, May 1944, 377
17. 603 Squadron Diary, 28:6:1942
18. Mario Roatta, *Otto Milioni di Baionette*, 210
19. The Memoirs of Field Marshal Kesselring, 122-125, 128-9
20. Ibid, 123
    B.H. Liddell Hart, *The Rommel Papers, 203*
    Stewart Perowne, *The Siege within The Walls*, 128-132, 145-6
21. Air Marshal Sir Hugh Lloyd, *Briefed to Attack, 223-224.*

9. JULY BATTLES AND A REMARKABLE ESCAPE

1. *Blackwood's Magazine*, May 1944, 384
2. Ibid, 377, 378
3. 603 Squadron Diary 1st July 1942
4. *Blackwood's Magazine*, May 1944, 378
5. 603 Squadron Diary, 2:7:1942
6. *Blackwood's Magazine*, May 1944, 378
7. Ibid, 378, 379
8. Ibid, 379
9. Letter from Tony Holland 18:12:1979
10. Public Record Office at Kew AIR 28/807, AIR 22/392
    Blackwood's Magazine, May 1944, 379
11. Ibid, 379, 380
12. *Blackwoods Magazine*, May 1944, 380
13. 608 Squadron Diary, 22:4:1942, 9:5:1942, 12:5:1942, 8:6:1942, 2:7:1942, 8:7:1942, 9:7:1942
14. *Blackwood's Magazine*, May 1944, 380

15. Public Record Office at Kew, Air 28/807, AIR 24/392
    603 Squadron Diary, 13:7:1942
    Blackwood's Magazine, May 1944, 382
16. Public Record Office at Kew, AIR 28/807
17. 603 Squadron Diary, 1:5:1942
18. Public Record Office at Kew, AIR 22/392
19. Ibid, AIR 22/392
20. Ibid, AIR 28/807
21. Ibid, AIR 28/807
    E. C. R. Baker, *The Fighter Aces of the RAF,* 139
    Leslie Hunt, *Twenty-one Squadrons, The History of the Royal Auxiliary Air Force 1925-1957,* 107
22. Public Record Office at Kew, AIR 28/807
23. Public Record Office at Kew, AIR 28/807
24. Letter from Group Captain Satchell DSO DFC dated 20:11:1979
25. Letter from Group Captain Cahill DSO DFC, dated 15:12:1979
26. *Blackwood's Magazine,* May 1944, 382
27. Ibid, 282
28. Ministry of Information: *The Air Battle of Malta,* 74
29. Public Record Office at Kew, PREM 3/266/5
30. The words in italics are added by the author, who obtained this detailed information from Ministry of Information: *The Air Battle of Malta,* 77, 78
31. *Blackwood's Magazine,* May 1944, 382
32. 603 Squadron Diary, 16:7:1942

10. THE CONVOY LIFELINE AND A FIGHTER OFFENSIVE

1. *Blackwood's Magazine,* May 1944, 382
2. Ibid, 382
3. Ibid, 383-384. See also Peter Shankland and Anthony Hunter, *Malta Convoy,* and Peter Smith, *Pedestal, The Malta Convoy, of August 1942*
4. Churchill, *The Second World War,* Vol. IV, 454
5. Public Record Office at Kew, PREM 3/266/2
6. Churchill, *The Second World War,* Vol. IV, 455
7. *Blackwood's Magazine,* May 1944, 384
8. Ibid, 384
9. Public Record Office at Kew, PREM 3/266/5
10. Letter from Wing Commander Paul Evans DFC 15:9:1942
11. Papers of Group Captain Arthur Donaldson DSO, DFC, AFC
12. Ibid
13. *Blackwood's Magazine,* May 1944, 384
14. Papers of Group Captain Arthur Donaldson DSO, DFC, AFC
15. Ministry of Information: *The Air Battle of Malta,* 86, 88, 89
16. Memoirs of Field Marshall Kesselring, 134, 135
17. Public Record Office at Kew, PREM 3/266/10A
18. Ibid
19. Sir John Wheeler-Bennett, *King George VI* (Macmillan & Co. Ltd 1958), 572

20. With the gracious permission of Her Majesty the Queen from the Royal Archives, the reference being RA G VI Box 3 ENV2
21. Public Record Office at Kew, PREM 3/266/10A

11. THE BREAKING OF THE LUFTWAFFE

1. Public Record Office at Kew, PREM 3/266/10A
2. Papers of Group Captain Arthur Donaldson DSO, DFC, AFC
   Papers of Air Vice Marshal Sandy Johnstone DFC
3. Ibid
4. Papers of Group Captain Arthur Donaldson DSO, DFC, AFC
5. Ibid
6. R. Leslie Oliver, *Malta Besieged*, 143
7. Public Record Office at Kew, AIR 28/807
8. Papers of Group Captain Arthur Donaldson DSO, AFC, AFC
   The Cabinet Minutes of 19 October 1942 (Public Record Office at Kew, CAB 65/28) state that over the previous seven days, Axis losses had been 102 destroyed, 45 probably destroyed and 111 damaged. RAF losses had been 34 fighters destroyed, but a number of the pilots had been saved. Group Captain Donaldson's figures for the whole period of the October onslaught are consistent with these figures.
9. Ministry of Information: *The Air Battle of Malta*, 93
10. Sir Arthur Bryant, *The Turn of the Tide*, 506-507
11. Ministry of Information: *The Air Battle of Malta*, 93
12. Memoirs of Field Marshal Kesselring, 129
13. Public Record Office at Kew, PREM 3/266/10A
14. General Playfair, *History of the Second World War*, Vol. III, 299
15. Papers of Laddie Lucas, CBE DSO DFC.

12. THE RAISING OF THE SIEGE AND THE CALL OF DUTY

1. Ministry of Information: *The Air Battle of Malta*, 94
2. Public Record Office at Kew, PREM 3/266/7
3. Ibid
4. Ian Cameron, *Red Duster, White Ensign*, 203, 204
   R. Leslie Oliver *Malta Besieged*, 149
   Ministry of Information: *The Air Battle of Malta*, 94
   See also Captain S.W. Roskill, *History of the Second World War*, Vol. II, *The War at Sea*
5. Ibid
6. Air Vice Marshal Sandy Johnstone DFC, *Where No Angels Dwell*, 119-120
7. R. Leslie Oliver, *Malta Besieged*, 150-153
8. Ibid, 170
9. Ibid, 172-173
10. Papers of Group Captain Arthur Donaldson DSO, DFC, AFC
11. R. Leslie Oliver, *Malta Besieged*, 163
12. Ibid, 171

13. Air Vice Marshal Sandy Johnstone, DFC, *Where No Angels Dwell*, 123-125

14. Papers of Air Vice Marshal Sandy Johnstone, DFC

15. R. Leslie Oliver, *Malta Besieged*, 146

16. Stewart Perowne, *The Siege within the Walls*, 181-182

17. George Hogan, *Malta, The Triumphant Years 1940-1943*, 166-7

18. Papers of Air Vice Marshal Sandy Johnstone DFC

19. Stewart Perowne, *The Siege within the Walls*, 145-146

20. B.H. Liddell Hart, *The Rommel Papers*, 288-289, See also Italian NLD Papers

21. Harold Macmillan, *The Blast of War 1939-45*, 349-50.

22. *The Times of Malta*, 21 June 1943

23. George Hogan, *Malta: The Triumphant Years*, 167-169
    Joseph Attard, *The Battle of Malta*, 232-235
    General Eisenhower, *Crusade in Europe*, 184
    Montgomery of El Alamein, *Memoirs*, 170-175

24. *The Times of Malta*, 5 August 1943

25. *The Times of Malta*, 17 August 1943

26. Harold Macmillan, *The Blast of War 1939-45*, 379-380, 384-390, 392

27. Joseph Attard, *The Battle of Malta*, 238-239

28. Winston Churchill, *The Second World War*, Vol. IV, *The Hinge of Fate*, 265

29. *The Times of Malta*, 11 December 1943

30. George Hogan, *Malta, The Triumphant Years*, 134
    Stephen Roskill, *The War at Sea*, Vol. II,, 227, 302-304, 430

31. See the account given by Major R.T. Gilchrist, in *Malta Strikes Back, The Story of 231 Infantry Brigade.*

32. Papers of Group Captain Arthur Donaldson DSO, DFC, AFC

33. See George Beurling and Leslie Roberts, *Malta Spitfire, The Story of a Fighter Pilot*

34. In the File at the Public Record Office at Kew, AIR 27/2028 and AIR 28/61 it is confirmed that they were sent out in Mosquito IX, MM 240 to photograph targets at Symphorien, Roman, Aspries Gap Tallard, Nice, La Californie, Moirans, Passy, Pont, De Navoy, Champagnole, Dijon area, St Dizier area. With the gift of hindsight it seems that this was an enormous amount for one sortie.

35. Letter from Sir Edward Brown, MBE, JP, dated 29.1.1980

36. Public Record Office at Kew, AIR, 27/2028 and AIR 28/61

37. Papers of Mrs. Brian Power

38. Ibid.

39. Public Record Office at Kew, AIR 27/2028

40. Letter from Air Vice Marshall Dodd, CBE, DSO, DFC, AFC, dated 5 August 1980

PART III

13. THE FIGHTER PILOTS AND THE VICTORY OF MALTA

1. Kenneth Poolman, *Faith, Hope and Charity, Three Planes Against an Air Force*, 197.

2. *Blackwood's Magazine*, May 1944, 233-235

3. Sybil Dobbie, *Grace Under Malta*, 9

4. George Hogan, *Malta: The Triumphant Years*, 126
5. I. McD. G. Stewart, *The Struggle for Crete, A Story of Lost Opportunity*, 476
6. J.A. Ritchie, (Bartimaeus), *Malta Invicta*, 32
7. Stewart Perowne, *The Siege within the Walls*, 128
8. Ministry of Information: *The Air Battle of Malta*, 95.

SELECT BIBLIOGRAPHY

PRIMARY SOURCES
I. The Diaries

The central part of the book is based upon the Squadron Diary of 603 (City of Edinburgh) Squadron, kept by Squadron Leader Lord David Douglas-Hamilton with the assistance of his Second-in-Command, Flight Lieutenant Bill Douglas. Whilst doing research, this diary was passed to the author by Mrs Diana Cameron, daughter of the late Bill Douglas, accompanied by a hand-written note of her father, for a friend, containing these words:

"Here is the Diary which David D-H and I kept as a record of our days in Malta from April till August 1942. David took it home—I did not get back till a month later—by some weeks the last of the band of 47 who took off from the "Wasp", which seemed an eternity before.

"It is pretty well a factual record . . . It contains little except a log of the basic events which affected us day by day. They were long days and hot . . . The action is there, but not the tension of waiting, the frustration of mechanical faults, or the miracle that our ground crews were able to get us safely airborne at all. Read it slowly for there is a lot to read between the lines.

"Nicholas Monsarrat got the background as near perfectly as one can recollect. The feeling of isolation— 1,000 miles to Gibraltar, another 1,000 to Alexandria, and 50 odd to Sicily . . .

"At home, the RAF Fighers were suffering heavy losses at the hands of the new F.W.190, and it was not until the Malta pilots filtered home that the highly successful and (then) sophisticated tactics we had developed to survive the odds, were gradually adopted and what had been unnecessary losses were reversed. In some ways then it was lucky for some of us to have missed that Summer at home, though we did not appreciate it at the time!

"I hope you will find it of interest—and will understand how it took a long time to go back to an island I now love.

"One more note—during all this, Imperial Airways never missed that nightly passenger service, alternately Gibraltar, Malta, Alexandria and reverse in a civilian Hudson."

A copy of this Diary is contained in "The Record of Service and Achievements of No. 603 (City of Edinburgh) Squadron, Royal Auxiliary Air Force" by Wing Commander J.L. Jack, MBE, MC, AE, and is available in the Imperial War Museum Library.

After his return from Malta, Squadron Leader Lord David Douglas-Hamilton completed his own personal Diary which was published in Blackwood's Magazine in two instalments, in April and May 1944, and it is available in many large Libraries.

While the Squadron Diary was a complete record of the activities of all the fighter pilots in the Squadron, David's personal Diary tells the story of the most critical phase of the Air Battle for Malta, from the point of view of a Spitfire Squadron Commander. Those Diaries were supplemented by the papers of his widow, Mrs Brian Power, compiled by his widow and his brother Malcolm.

Also, the late Group Captain Arthur Donaldson DSO DFC AFC had written a Diary covering the final confrontation with the Luftwaffe. It was destroyed when the Liberator taking him to Gibraltar crashed into the sea. Years later he wrote down his recollections of what he believed to be the three most important months of his life, as the Wing Leader in charge of Fighter operations at Takali aerodrome, and he saw and approved his eye-witness account as given in this book.

II. The Royal Archives

1. The Report of Field Marshal Lord Gort VC to King George VI, after presenting the George Cross in Malta is contained in RA GVI Box 3 Env 2 of the Royal Archives at Windsor.

Other full and relevant reports of the ceremony were given in the Times of Malta, both at the time of the original award by the King, and at the time of the later ceremony in Malta.

III. Public Record Office at Kew

The most significant series of documents relating to Malta during the most intense part of the Siege are contained in the Prime Minister's Files PREM3/266/1-8 and in PREM3/266/10A.

PREM3/266/1 deals in some detail with the resons for the appointment of General Gort VC as Governor in Malta.

PREM3/266/2 covers the period from January to November 1942, and confirms that the Chiefs of Staff and Prime Minister regarded Malta as being so vital as an air staging point, as well as being "an impediment to enemy reinforcements", that "the most dramatic steps" were in order to sustain the island fortress by convoys, however considerable the price.

PREM3/266/3 contains General Dobbie's appreciation of the need to defend Gozo as well as Malta, and his assessment of Malta's importance as a base for offensive operations against Axis communications between Italy and North Africa.

PREM3/266/4 has a summary of the evidence of bomb damage sustained by the aerodromes in Malta, after the Spitfires of the First USS Wasp Relief Force had landed, and the results of the return of the USS Wasp with HMS Eagle on 9 May 1942.

PREM3/266/5 has an interesting Report from the Governor Lord Gort VC to the Prime Minister on the situation in Malta at the end of July 1942.

PREM3/266/6 deals with the subject of evacuating civilians from Malta.

PREM3/266/7 raises the subject of Malta's War Damage, and the British Government's gift of £10,000,000 for the purpose of restoration and rebuilding.

PREM3/266/8 contains a note sent on the Prime Minister's behalf that he no longer wished to receive the daily Malta air operational summary.

PREM3 /266/10A relates to the feeding of Malta with Spitfires to obtain and maintain air supremacy, the likelihood and scale and method of Axis attack on Malta, the nature of the food position, and the need to make all possible economies of petrol.

2. The Cabinet Minutes and Documents, which can be traced on the open shelves, contain much relevant information.

IV. Air Ministry Files

Some of the most interesting Air Ministry files are AIR 20/914m AIR 20/2428, AIR 24/908 and AIR 24/909.

AIR 20/914 deals with the need to have experienced pilots in Malta. AIR 20/2428 relates to the return of the USS Wasp to relieve Malta, and the recovery of air supremacy. AIR/24/908 and 909 deal with the scale of Axis attacks on Malta and the attacks made by Malta-based aircraft on Axis shipping.

The various Operations Record Books were also valuable as source, including that of 603 Squadron before leaving for Malta, AIR 27/2079, that of Takali Aerodrome in 1942, AIR 28/807, the Intelligence Summaries of Takali being AIR 22/392, The Operations Record Books of 544 Squadron were AIR 27/2024, AIR 27/2028 and AIR 27/2031.

V. Memoirs, Diaries and Secondary Works, containing or making use of original material.

Attard, Joseph, *The Battle of Malta*, William Kimber & Co. Ltd. 1980.

Austin, Dennis, *Malta and the End of Empire,* Frank Cass & Co. Ltd. 1971.

Austin, J. *Grand Barrage,* Hodder & Stoughton, 1944.

Baker, E. C. R. *The Figher Aces of the RAF 1939-1945,* William Kimber & Co. Ltd. 1962.

Barnham, Denis, *One Man's Window,* William Kimber & Co. Ltd. 1956.

Bekker, Cajus, *Luftwaffe War Diaries,* Macdonald & Co. Ltd. 1967.

Beurling, George, and Robert, Leslie, *Malta Spitfire, The*

Story of a Fighter Pilot, Arms and Armour Press 1973.

Blouet, Brian, *The Story of Malta,* London, Faber & Faber 1979.

Bondin, Ray, *Deportation 1942, The Internment and Deportation of Maltese Nationalists,* Malta 1980.

Brennan, Paul and Hesselyn, Ray, *Spitfires over Malta,* Jarrolds 1943.

Brookes, Andrew, *Photo Reconnaisance,* Ian Allan Ltd., 1975.

Bryant, Sir Arthur, *Turn of the Tide,* Collins 1957.

Cameron, Ian, *Red Duster, White Ensign, The Story of the Malta Convoys,* Frederick Muller Ltd. 1959.

Churchill, Sir Winston, *The Second World War,* vols. I-VI, Cassell & Co. Ltd.

Churchill, Sir Winston, *Secret Session Speeches,* compiled by Charles Wade, Cassell & Co. Ltd.

Ciano Diaries, American translation, Heinemann 1947.

Coccia, Aldo, *Submarines Attacking,* William Kimber & Co. Ltd. 1956.

Colville, J.R., *Man of Valour, Field Marshall Lord Gort VC,* Collins 1972.

Connell, John, *Auchinleck,* Cassell 1964.

Dean, Sir Maurice, *The Royal Air Force and Two World Wars,* Cassell & Co. Ltd. 1979.

Dobbie, Sybil, *Grace under Malta,* Lindsay-Drummond 1944.

Dobbie, Sybil, *Faith and Fortitude, The Life and work of Sir William Dobbie,* 1980 by Johnston.

Eisenhower, General, *Crusade in Europe,* Heinemann 1948

Gerard, Francis, *Malta Magnificent,* Cassell & Co. Ltd. 1943.

Gilchrist, Major R.T. *Malta Strikes Back, The Story of 231 Infantry Brigade,* Gale and Polden Ltd 1946.

Gorlitz, Walter, *The Memoirs of Field Marshal Keitel,* William Kimber 1965.

Gretton, Vice Admiral Sir Peter, *Convoy Escort Commander,* Cassell & Company Ltd 1964.

Guedella, Philip, *Middle East 1940-1942, A Study in Air Power,* Hodder & Stoughton 1944.

Hart, B.A. Liddell, *The Rommel Papers,* Collins 1953.

Hay, Ian, *The Unconquered Isle, The Story of Malta GC,* Hodder & Stoughton, 1943.

Hitler's Table Talk, Introduction by Professor Hugh Trevor-Roper, Weidenfeld & Nicolson 1953.

Hitler's War Directives, edited by Professor Hugh Trevor-Roper, Sidgwick & Jackson 1964.

Hogan, G. *Malta: The Triumphant Years,* R. Hale 1979.

Holman, Gordon, *In Danger's Hour,* Hodder & Stoughton, 1948.

Hunt, Leslie, *Twenty-one Squadrons, The History of the Royal Air Force 1925-1957.*

Ismay, Lord, *Memoirs,* Heinemann.

Jackson, R. *Malta History, Yeoman on the George Cross Island,* London, A. Baker 1980

Jackson, W. G. F. *The Battle for Italy,* BT Batsford Ltd 1947

Jacobsen, H. A. and Rohwehr J, *Decisive Battles of World War II, The German View,* Andre Deutsch 1965.

Johnstone, Johnny, *Tattered Battlements, A Malta Diary by a Fighter Pilot,* Peter Davies 1943

Johnstone, Air Vice Marshal Sandy, CB DFC
  Where No Angels Dwell, Harrolds 1969
  Enemy in the Sky, Presidio Press 1978
  Adventure in the Sky, William Kimber 1978.

Kesselring, Field Marshal, *Memoirs,* William Kimber 1953

Lloyd, Air Vice Marshal Sir Hugh P. *Briefed to Attack, Malta's Part in African Victory,* Hodder & Stoughton 1949.

Lucas, Laddie, *Five Up,* Sidgwick & Jackson 1978

Macmillan, Harold, *The Blast of War,* Macmillan 1967

Manvell, Roger and Fraenkel, Heinrich, *Hermann Goering,* Heinemann 1962

March, Edgar J., *The British Destroyer,* Seeley Service 1968

Mars, Alastair, *Unbroken,* Muller 1953

Ministry of Information, *Air Battle of Malta, The Official Account of the RAF in Malta, June 1940 to November 1942,* HMSO 1944.

Montgomery, Field Marshal Viscount, *Memoirs,* Collins 1958.

Mosley, Leonard, *The Reich Marshal, A Biography of Goering,* Doubleday 1974

Norman, Kathleen, *For Gallantry, Malta's Story by a Naval Wife,* Arthur Stockwell Ltd 1956

Oliver, R. Leslie, *Malta at Bay, An Eye Witness Account,* Hodder & Stoughton 1970.

Phillips, C.E. Lucas, *Alamein,* Heinemann 1962.

Playfair, Major-General, *The Mediterranean and Middle East,* Vol. III and IV, *History of the Second World War,* HMSO 1960.

Poolman, Kenneth, *Faith Hope and Charity, Three Planes against an Air Force,* William Kimber 1954.

  Night Strike from Malta, 830 Squadron RN and Rommel's Convoys, London, Jane's, 1980.

Pope, Dudley, *Flag 4, The Battle of Coastal Forces in the Mediterranean,* William Kimber 1954.

Popham, Hugh, *Sea Flight,* William Kimber 1956.

Ramsey, Winston G. *After the Battle, Malta GC Number 10,* published by Battle of Britain Prints International Ltd 1975.

Richards, Dennis and St George Saunders, Hilary, *Royal Air Force 1939-1945* HMSO 1957.

Ritchie, J.A. *Malta Invicta,* Chatto & Windus, 1943.

Ritchie Captain Lewis, *The Epic of Malta,* Odham's Press Ltd 1943.

Roatto, Mario, *Otto Milioni di Baionette,* Mondadori.

Roskill, Captain S.W. *War at Sea* Vols I and II HMSO 1956-1960 *A Merchant Fleet at War,* Collins 1962.

Ruge, Vice Admiral Sir Frederick, *Sea Warfare,* Cassell 1957.

Shankland, Peter and Hunter, Anthony, *Malta Convoy,* Collins 1961

Ships Company, Our Penelope, Guild Books 1943.

Smith, Peter C. Pedestal, *The Malta Convoy of August 1943,* William Kimber 1970

  The Battles of the Malta Sailing Forces, Ian Allen 1974.

  The Stuka at War, Ian Allan 1971.

Stewart, I McD G, *The Struggle for Crete 20 May-June 1941, A Story of Lost Opportunity,* Oxford University Press 1966

Strickland, Mabel, *A Collection of Essays on Malta 1923-1954,* Progress Press Co. Ltd. Malta

Times of Malta.
Vian Admiral Sir Philip, *Action this Day,* Muller 1960.
Webster, Sir Charles and Frankland, Noble, *The Strategic Air Offensive against Germany 1939-1945,* vols II and III of *History of the Second World War,* HMSO 1961.
Weldon, Lt. Col. HEC *Drama in Malta* Gale 1947.
Wheeler-Bennett, Sir John, *King George VI,* Macmillan & Co. Ltd. 1958.
Young, Desmond, *Rommel,* Collins 1950.

A work of Fiction, giving a picture of the atmosphere in war-time Malta is *The Kappillan of Malta* by Nicholas Monsarrat, published by Pan Books in 1975.

Index

205